Advanced Placement English

Practical Approaches to Literary Analysis

Mary Anne Kovacs
Jo Reed
Shirley H. Strobel

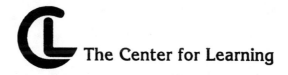
The Center for Learning

Mary Anne Kovacs, coauthor of curriculum units in the English and social studies series, earned her M.A. at the Bread Loaf School of English, Middlebury College, VT.

Jo Reed, a secondary Language Arts instructor, earned her M.S. in Education from Kansas State University's Department of Curriculum and Instruction.

Shirley H. Strobel earned her M.A. from Duke University. She has served as editor of an educators' magazine and has authored The Center for Learning novel/drama unit *The Brothers Karamazov*.

The Publishing Team
Rose Schaffer, M.A., President/Chief Executive Officer
Bernadette Vetter, M.A., Vice President
Diane Podnar, M.S., Production Director

Cover Design
Robin Smith

Advanced Placement English: Practical Approaches to Literary Analysis is a revision of the 1984 Center for Learning publication *Advanced Placement English: Challenging Approaches for Honors, Gifted, and AP English Classes.*

List of credits found on Acknowledgments Page beginning on 219.

ISBN 1-56077-532-7

Contents

Introduction

The following materials and exercises for teachers and students have been designed according to several assumptions about gifted students and Advanced Placement or Honors English classes.

Teaching the talented can be a delight. It can also be a difficult challenge! No less than their peers, highly capable students tire of strictly read-discuss-write academic programs. At the same time, they often reject the too-cute. They can, however, thrive on a varied, intellectually stimulating program geared toward developing their powers of analysis and synthesis to the highest possible level. The universal concerns of literature also contribute to the growth of empathetic hearts and keen minds.

The purpose of the Advanced Placement program is to provide talented high school seniors with college-level courses. The Advanced Placement examinations given in May of each year provide a standardized method of evaluating students' achievements and reporting them to colleges. The Advanced Placement examinations include both objective and essay sections, and they change from year to year so that they always challenge students' abilities. The examinations stress analytic skills, ability to synthesize, ability to "think on their feet," and composition skills.

Advanced Placement and Honors classes generally consist of talented and highly motivated students. For many the goal is a high score on an Advanced Placement examination, enabling them to test out of the freshman college English courses. Others are more interested in the experience of a high-powered English study or in being in class with others who are also serious about learning. Regardless of the students' varying short term goals, the teacher can successfully help everyone in the class by providing a stimulating atmosphere through activities that challenge students' logic, creativity, insight, and technical skills. Most effective Advanced Placement programs focus primarily on developing these abilities, rather than on attempting to "teach to" the Advanced Placement examinations.

The materials in this unit are designed to help teachers incorporate extra challenge and enjoyment into Advanced Placement, Honors, and Gifted English classes. The unit has the following general objectives:

1. To enable students to analyze poems, short stories, nonfiction, drama, and novels independently

2. To equip students with skills in stylistic analysis of prose passages

3. To enable students to write effective critical analyses

4. To enable students to complete well-written, timed compositions on impromptu subjects

5. To have students probe themes as they are evidenced in a variety of works

6. To enable students to synthesize treatments of specific themes

Teacher Notes

Using the Course Materials

This book consists of teacher lesson plans and student handouts for thirty-nine lessons. The lessons included reflect only the special challenge objectives of an Advanced Placement or Honors course. More basic educational approaches to the genres, composition, and major literary traditions are available through a variety of other Center for Learning texts.

Each lesson is designed for a tightly compressed class period, including effective preliminary and follow-up work. Many lessons lend themselves to expansion to two or three class days. The handouts, numbered for quick reference, are intended for distribution to students. Students are encouraged to keep handouts in an organized notebook or folder for reference during succeeding lessons. Answers to handouts will vary unless otherwise indicated.

This unit is divided into two sections. The first focuses on in-depth analysis of each of the five genres. The second leads students to synthesis along thematic lines.

Because each lesson represents a special extra-challenge extension to the regular English curriculum, the lessons do not incorporate specific assignments linking each lesson to the next. Assignments are described in notes to the teacher when they serve as necessary background for a given class. They appear within the procedure when they are primarily introductory or follow-up material.

Teaching Approaches

Because peer group interaction is important in the learning process, many activities in this unit involve students in working with each other to fulfill specific goals. Because Advanced Placement classes are often rather small and students frequently have come to know one another very well, allowing flexibility in group formation may be better than assigning regular partners or small groups.

Equally important is your interaction with students in a large group, in small groups, and on a one-to-one basis. Frequency and variety of opportunities for interaction facilitate learning and promote a confident educational atmosphere.

Evaluation

Evaluation of student achievement in the Advanced Placement course can be accomplished in several ways. Individual handouts provide daily means of checking on students' progress. Critical essays and timed writings help to gauge students' growth in analysis and composition skills. While results of the May Advanced Placement examinations are not available until midsummer, too late for end-of-the-year grading, they are an invaluable tool for evaluating both individual students and the program itself.

Part 1
Analysis

Advanced Placement and Honors students are usually eager for the opportunity to go beyond understanding and application exercises to in-depth analysis. The lessons in the first part of this resource unit provide activities and materials designed to enable students to analyze significant literary works in each of the five genres.

Readily available and easily read, short stories afford a wide variety of settings, characters, conflicts, themes, and styles. In addition, the concise structure and relative simplicity of plot and characters facilitate students' rapid development of basic analytic dexterity. For these reasons, this course begins with analysis of short stories.

The second group of lessons leads students to effective poem analysis. The intensity, which is the hallmark of good poetry, results from tightly compressed language. Thus, the study of poems often challenges even very bright students. The lessons in this section help to generate students' confidence, as well as to demonstrate that poetry can enlarge one's experience of life.

The human need for self-expression and sharing of experiences often expresses itself through nonfictional prose, the subject of the third section. Here the subject matter is endless, the attitudes limitless; here, too, the reader needs analytic skills that facilitate an accurate assessment of a writer's purposes, authority, logic, and implications.

The fourth section focuses on the three great ages of drama: The Golden Age of Greece, Shakespeare's England, and the modern theatre. Drama has a unique way of reflecting the beliefs, doubts, and longings of men and women; it mirrors the atmosphere of the age from which it emerges. Advanced Placement students are challenged to a greater understanding of the conflicts, failures, and victories that comprise the human experience.

Finally, the novel, because of its length and complexity, offers a special challenge, along with many opportunities for analysis and insight. Great novels provide long and deep looks at individual people's lives and the human experience in general. The fifth section equips students with tools for and practice in analyzing these great works.

1

Lesson 1
Elements of Fiction

Objective

- To enable students to develop skills in analysis and use the terminology appropriate to the short story

Notes to the Teacher

The short story has its roots in the oral tradition of literature and derives from a basic creative desire to tell and hear stories. The short story is a unique genre, differing from tale in its formal development and from novel in its limited development. The short story, upon careful analysis, is the result of unity in its elements.

In this lesson, students review the elements of the short story and apply them to William Carlos Williams's "The Use of Force." A doctor himself, Williams situates the story in the framework of a doctor-patient relationship.

You will want to obtain the short story and make it available to your class. Students may read the story in preparation of the lesson, or you may want them to read it in class.

Procedure

1. Use **Handout 1** to review the elements of fiction. Advanced Placement students may not need to spend valuable class time in extensive review of these terms. However, further lessons are based on the terminology on the handout.

2. Have students read "The Use of Force" during class if they have not already read it in preparation for class.

3. Ask students to apply each of the literary terms on **Handout 1** to "The Use of Force." **Suggested Responses:**

   Setting—*a house call in the kitchen of the patient's home*

   Characters—*family named Olson, consisting of a father, mother, and little girl named Mathilda, who is ill; a doctor, unnamed*

Plot—*After being summoned by the child's mother, the doctor makes a house call to determine the nature of Mathilda's illness. Mathilda refuses to open her mouth for examination and diagnosis. A brutal battle ensues, and finally, the doctor is successful in opening her mouth and discovers her diseased tonsils, which indicate diphtheria. External conflict (doctor vs. child, health vs. sickness) as well as internal (doctor's professionalism vs. his delight in hurting the child)*

Theme—*When conflict is reduced to power vs. weakness, power triumphs; when authority decides to conquer a situation, resistance capitulates; sometimes pain is a prelude to cure.*

Point of View—*first person, major character (doctor as narrator)*

Style—*no use of quotation marks in dialogue; contrast of physical description of Mathilda with her savageness; Williams creates a doctor whose honesty in describing his experience with the little girl reveals his pleasure in and regret for the confrontation.*

Tone—*begins with concern for social welfare, shifts to violence, abuse, hostility*

Irony—*ambivalence between doctor's professionalism and his brutality*

Symbolism—*not immediately evident in this story, although some students may perceive the ordeal as a bodily violation*

Elements of Fiction

Setting   The background against which the story takes place is referred to as *setting*. This includes such factors as geographical location, placement of physical objects, and the time or period in which the action occurs. The emotional environment of the characters (religious, social, etc.) can also be used in the analysis of setting.

Character   Fictional characters are developed through description, actions, thoughts, and speeches, direct statement from the writer, and/or opinions voiced by other characters. Depending on their importance in the story, characters are developed to different degrees. Characters can be identified as *static*, meaning they undergo no changes in the story, or *dynamic*, meaning that a permanent change, for better or worse, in personality, outlook, or some other aspect of character occurs within the framework of the short story. The effectiveness of the writer's development of characters correlates with the emotional response of the reader.

Plot   *Plot* can be defined as the pattern that results from the events in the story in the order in which they are presented. Most plots involve conflict, external and/or internal, as characters participate in a series of actions. In some stories, plot may not be the emphasis; the author may instead use revelation, in which the character or reader moves toward a particular insight or understanding.

Theme   This term refers to the central idea or dominating thought, which results from the other elements contained in fiction. Theme may be a complex, abstract concept, but one which summarizes the author's purpose in writing the narrative.

Point of View   The vantage point from which the author presents the action of the story is called *point of view*. Point of view encompasses voice, involvement, knowledge, and reliability. The main types of point of view are described below:

- Third person, omniscient—The narrator is an outside observer who never refers to himself/herself as "I," "me," or "we." This narrator has unlimited access to all characters and knows everything that all of the characters do, think, see, and feel.
- Third person, limited omniscient—The narrator's knowledge of thoughts, actions, visual perceptions, and feelings is limited to one or a few characters.
- Third person, objective—The narrator becomes a camera, recording actions and behaviors without comment or interpretation. This narrator cannot record thoughts or feelings.
- First person—A character (either major or minor) refers to himself/herself as "I" while telling the story. This narrator's knowledge is limited to personal interpretations, observations, and experiences.

Authors are not restricted to these main types of point of view, and they may use combinations or may experiment with various methods of storytelling.

Style   Style is a product of the unique conscious and unconscious choices that an author makes concerning sentence structure, setting, subject matter, tone, and numerous other elements of fiction.

Tone   *Tone* refers to the manner of speaking that an author uses. An author's tone may be revealed in the attitude toward the characters and subject, the construction of sentence patterns, word usage, figurative language, or any number of other literary devices. By controlling tone, an author creates spirit and attitude.

Irony   Irony in literature is usually differentiated into three main categories. *Verbal irony* is that which occurs when what is said contrasts with what is meant. *Dramatic irony* is the discrepancy between what the author says and what the reader knows is true. *Irony of situation* illustrates the disparity between what is and what is logically expected. The contrasts generated by the use of irony add dimension to the theme of a story.

Symbolism   *Symbolism* is the literal use of an object, person, action, or other item that suggests a larger, perhaps more universal, meaning. For example, a character's voyage may be used to suggest a journey through life, or the use of water within a story may suggest a cleansing through spiritual rebirth.

Lesson 2
Analysis of Conflict for Theme

Objective

- To enable students to create a theme statement for a narrative by analysis of the narrative's conflict

Notes to the Teacher

A crucial part of the process of independent analysis is conceptualization of theme. Although the central meaning of some stories is easily ascertained, others give students considerable difficulty. Through a rather simple seven-step process for the analysis of conflict, each student can be taught to arrive at a statement of theme.

The way in which an author does or does not resolve conflict is the clearest indication of theme. Even in narratives where the conflict is not resolved but only revealed, theme grows out of the reader's understanding of why the conflict is not resolved.

The assumption behind this kind of conflict analysis is that all conflicts within the well-written story, novel, or play are developed to demonstrate an essential idea. Often an exterior conflict encountered by the protagonist is mirrored by an interior conflict. In addition, minor characters usually reflect the major conflict in one of its several forms. When the abstract ideas behind these conflicts are identified, and when the resolution of the conflict is examined, the theme of the story becomes apparent.

You will want to obtain the short story "The Japanese Quince" and make it available to your class.* Students may read the story in preparation of the lesson, or you may want them to read it in class.

Procedure

1. Point out to students that a short story is like a string of beads. It contains many elements (techniques) all strung together by an idea, called the theme, the most significant single element of a story.

2. Work through **Handout 2** with students to demonstrate the process of conflict analysis as it applies to "The Use of Force."
   Suggested Responses:
   1. *Conflict in terms of characters*

      Doctor vs. Mathilda

      Father vs. Mathilda

      Mother vs. Mathilda

      Parents vs. Doctor
   2. *Inner conflict is present.*

      Doctor vs. Doctor

      When the doctor finds himself having "fallen in love with the savage brat" so that "the parents were contemptible to me," part of him has joined forces with the girl.
   3. Turning point—*Doctor forces the girl's mouth open so he can see her infected throat, but in doing so, he becomes as savage as she is.*

      Major conflict—*Doctor vs. Doctor*
   4. *Encourage the class to generate as many possibilities as they can (the more ideas, the richer the understanding of the story). For each of the abstractions suggested, ask the student to supply a detail from the story that supports it. You may wish to ask for evidence only in the case of doubt.*

      Abstract ideas will apply both to the inner and outer conflicts, but inner conflict is demonstrated here, since it is the most subtle.

Calm	vs.	Fury
"I told the parents it was entirely up to them."		*"I had grown furious at a child."*

Health	vs.	Sickness
Doctor explores his own savagery.		*Doctor is infected by brutal feelings.*

Reason	vs.	Passion
"You're old enough to understand what I am saying."		*Doctor attacks child "in a final unreasoning assault."*

* "The Japanese Quince" can be found in Perrine's *Story and Structure* (Harcourt Brace Jovanovich).

7

Social Good	*vs.*	**Individual Will**	
"Others must be protected against her. It is a social necessity."		*"It was a pleasure to attack her."*	

Love	*vs.*	**Hate**
"I'd already fallen in love with the savage brat."		*"I could have torn the child apart in my own fury and enjoyed it."*

Victory	*vs.*	**Defeat**
"There it was—both tonsils covered with membrane."		*"A feeling of adult shame bred of a longing for muscular release . . ."*

5. *Individual will, passion, and fury win; the doctor's sickness takes over temporarily, but his honesty in judging his own actions opens the way to his mental health and recovery of the positive side of his character.*

6. *The doctor's fury and brutality win because in this desperate battle he cannot control them, perhaps because he does not recognize that he is capable of such feelings. The recognition he arrives at in the story is a victory since in the next battle he will be more capable of control.*

7. *Possible theme statements*

   Even people with the best intentions may find themselves responding with savage fury in a desperate situation.

   An honest examination of one's responses in a desperate situation may reveal unwelcome depths of brutality.

3. Have students read "The Japanese Quince" by John Galsworthy and work through the conflict analysis in **Handout 2** in pairs.

   Suggested Responses:

   1. *Conflict in terms of characters*

      Mr. Nilson   vs. Japanese quince

      In this story, the title signals that the Japanese quince rather than a person becomes the antagonist.

      Mr. Nilson   vs.   Mr. Tandram

   2. *Inner conflict is present.*

      Mr. Nilson   vs.   Mr. Nilson

   3. Turning point—*Mr. Nilson goes inside because he sees himself mirrored in Mr. Tandram who "looked a little foolish."*

      Main conflict—*Mr. Nilson vs. Japanese quince*

The main and secondary conflicts interlock at the turning point, but the title indicates which is the major one.

4. *Abstract ideas in conflict*

Conformity	*vs.*	**Potentiality**
"Mr. Tandram looked a little foolish," and Mr. Nilson felt as though "he had seen himself."		*Spring, "feeling of emptiness"*

Death	*vs.*	**New Life**
"Unaccountably upset, Mr. Nilson turned abruptly into the house . . ."		*Japanese quince*

Routine	*vs.*	**Freedom**
Morning paper, half an hour to breakfast		*Blackbird*

Rigidity	*vs.*	**Spontaneity**
"Being married," he had not yet had the occasion to speak to his neighbor of five years.		*A blackbird burst into song.*

Drabness	*vs.*	**Beauty**
Black frock coat		*"The little tree was so alive and pretty!"*

Sobriety	*vs.*	**Exuberance**
"He had scarcely made two revolutions" on the circular garden path.		*A blackbird burst into song.*

Closed	*vs.*	**Open**
His neighbor of five years was a stranger.		*"Nice fellow . . . I rather like him."*

Uniformity	*vs.*	**Uniqueness**
The two men are mirror images.		*Japanese quince, blackbird*

Note that students might rearrange the order in which they have listed Mr. Nilson and Mr. Tandram in order to reveal Mr. Nilson's inner conflict. Mr. Nilson views Mr. Tandram as the rigid, closed person, while he sees himself as unique and free. This shift points out the irony that Mr. Nilson wants to be different from his neighbor, but he is afraid to leave his financial rut to become alive to the beauty of spring.

5. *Rigidity and conformity win.*

6. *Mr. Nilson is afraid of looking ridiculous.*

7. *Possible theme statements*

   Exciting possibilities for personal renewal may be passed up because of a fear of appearing ridiculous. Fear may close off the opportunity for spontaneity and exuberant living.

4. If time permits, examine other elements of the story that reinforce the theme.

a. Symbolism

Japanese quince—blooming represents rebirth

Blackbird—appearance parallels the black frock coats of the two men but symbolizes the potential for exuberant living for them

Names—*Nilson* literally means "son of nothing." *Tandram* plays on two puns: first, "humdrum," and second, "tandem" (or double).

Path—circle represents repetitious life

b. Irony

The tree that seems more than a tree contrasts with the men that are less than men.

Analyzing Conflict for Theme

This sheet will help you derive a theme statement through an analysis of a narrative's conflict.

1. State the conflict in terms of characters who are in conflict in the narrative. List all possible conflicts in the following form:

   Character 1   vs.   Character 2

   (i.e., Tom vs. Joe; Tom vs. Tornado)

2. Is there an inner conflict within the protagonist? If yes, add protagonist vs. protagonist (Tom vs. Tom).

3. Mark with an * the major conflict, other than the inner conflict, in the story. To identify this conflict correctly, identify the climax or turning point in the narrative. Which conflict is at issue at this point?

   Turning point—

   Major conflict—

4. For each of the conflicts listed in step 1, identify the ideas it represents, as paired opposites of abstractions (i.e., love vs. duty). Rearrange, if necessary, the order in which you have listed characters so that all characters who represent the same type of abstract idea appear on the same side of the word "vs."

5. Does one side of the conflict win over the other by the end of the narrative? If yes, which side wins?

6. If you answered step 5 with "yes," why did that side win?

   If you answered step 5 with "no," why was no resolution possible?

7. Your answer to step 6 should lead directly to a theme statement. Write it out, remembering to do the following:

   a. Express the theme in general terms, avoiding reference to any particular character. You may use a social role, such as "mother" or an age bracket, such as "adolescent."

   b. Express the theme in a complete statement. "The innocence of a child" is the topic, not the theme.

   c. If your theme statement is complex and contains subordinate clauses or phrases, be sure the important idea is in the main clause.

Lesson 3
Analyzing Carson McCullers's "The Jockey"

Objective

- To enable students to analyze a tightly compressed and highly unified short story

Notes to the Teacher

While some stories readily lend themselves to theme identification and character interpretation, others are more subtle. Close attention to point of view, tone, details, symbols, and other literary devices can help students to come to terms with these challenging short stories.

In this lesson, students analyze Carson McCullers's "The Jockey," a tightly compressed treatment of a timeless theme, the individual's helplessness in a conflict with a social system. Before you begin this lesson, you will want to make the story available to your students to read.* **Handout 3** is to be completed after the story has been read.

Procedure

1. Use **Handout 3** to have students share their initial impressions of and perceptions about "The Jockey."

   Suggested Responses:
   2. *Details reflect his colorful, clown-like attire contrasting with his pinched, gray, still body.*
   3. *The men are large and powerful; throughout the story, they are eating.*
   4. *His friend, McGuire, was recently crippled in a horse race accident.*
   5. *A libertine is a person who is not restrained by moral limits.*
   6. *Bitsy Barlow vs. the three men*
   7. *The little man is powerless, capable only of futile gestures, in his conflict with The System.*

2. Point out that food and colors are important motifs in "The Jockey." Ask half the class to scan the story for all food references and the other half to list all color references.

3. Have students work with partners to write short statements describing the significance of the food or color imagery.

4. Have students share their conclusions.

   Suggested Responses:
   The food imagery accentuates the contrast between the isolated jockey and the three men.
   The gray jockey contrasts with his own bright clothing, as well as with the red associated with the dining room and the three men.

5. Ask students the following questions:

   a. Why does Carson McCullers include the line, "Everyone was with somebody else; there was no other person drinking alone that night?"
   This line is a direct statement of the jockey's total isolation in this social environment.

   b. Why does Bitsy Barlow chew up and spit out the French-fried potatoes at the end?
   This childish gesture expresses the jockey's futile rage, as well as his rejection of the world of the three men.

   c. Why are those men silent at the end?
   The silence may reflect embarrassment; on the other hand, it may show that Bitsy's rage is unable to touch the rich and powerful.

6. Ask students to identify and evaluate the point of view used in the story.
   Combination of third person, objective, with occasional third person, limited omniscient,

* "The Jockey" can be found in *50 Great Short Stories* (Bantam Books).

reflects the story's main concerns. Bitsy Barlow can have very little effect on his objective environment.

7. Ask students the following questions:

   a. In what ways do the jockey and the three men seem to be symbols?

      The jockey represents all people who are "little" in the sense of being powerless; the three men represent corporate power and wealth.

   b. Why, then, does the conflict in the story remain unresolved?

      The conflict between the little individual and The System is an ongoing one. Leaving the story's conflict unresolved is realistic.

8. Remind students that a critical essay can focus on any significant element(s) of a literary work. Ask them to compose possible thesis statements for a critical essay that could be written about "The Jockey."

Example—In "The Jockey," Carson McCullers effectively uses food imagery to point out the impotence of the little individual in conflict with The System.

Name_____

Date _____

Carson McCullers's "The Jockey"

1. Describe your initial response to this story.

2. Reread the first two paragraphs, and underline all details describing the jockey's appearance.

3. How do the three men differ from the jockey?

4. What past event seems to have caused Bitsy Barlow's anger?

5. What is a *libertine*?

6. Identify the central conflict.

7. State a theme conveyed by the story.

Lesson 4
Group Work in Short Story Analysis

Objective

- To allow students the opportunity to work in groups as they discover elements within a particular short story

Notes to the Teacher

You may adjust the time required for this lesson by assigning the reading of the stories as homework. At the right is a suggested list of short stories to use for this lesson, although there are many others of equal literary value.

Procedure

1. Divide students into small groups of two or three.

2. Assign a short story to each group. Allow time for reading the story before beginning work.

3. Distribute a single copy of **Handout 4** to each group. Ask students to complete the handout as it applies to their stories.

4. After work on handouts is completed, ask groups to form a panel and present their findings to the remainder of the class.

5. Students should be prepared to support their conclusions by citing specific examples from the stories.

Suggested short stories for use in this lesson

"Silent Snow, Secret Snow"
    Conrad Aiken
"Hands"
    Sherwood Anderson
"An Occurrence at Owl Creek Bridge"
    Ambrose Bierce
"Tears, Idle Tears"
    Elizabeth Bowen
"Like a Bad Dream"
    Henrik Böll
"The Guest"
    Albert Camus
"Paul's Case"
    Willa Cather
"The Kiss"
    Anton Chekhov
"The Lagoon"
    Joseph Conrad
"A Rose for Emily"
    William Faulkner
"A Woman with a Past"
    F. Scott Fitzgerald
"The Other Side of the Hedge"
    E. M. Forster
"Putois"
    Anatole France
"The Destructors"
    Graham Greene
"Hills Like White Elephants"
    Ernest Hemingway
"Eveline"
    James Joyce
"Haircut"
    Ring Lardner
"The Horse Dealer's Daughter"
    D. H. Lawrence
"Through the Tunnel"
    Doris Lessing
"The Sojourner"
    Carson McCullers

"Garden Party"
    Katherine Mansfield
"The Silver Crown"
    Bernard Malamud
"A Good Man Is Hard to Find"
    Flannery O'Connor
"Man of the House"
    Frank O'Connor
"The Sniper"
    Liam O'Flaherty
"Theft"
    Katherine Anne Porter
"Defender of the Faith"
    Philip Roth
"The Open Window"
    Saki (H. H. Munro)
"For Esmè—With Love and Squalor"
    J. D. Salinger
"The Eighty-Yard Run"
    Irwin Shaw
"The Little Shoemakers"
    Isaac Singer
"How Beautiful with Shoes"
    Wilbur Daniel Steele
"The Chrysanthemums"
    John Steinbeck
"The Phoenix"
    Sylvia Townsend Warner
"Blackberry Winter"
    Robert Penn Warren
"The Worn Path"
    Eudora Welty
"Roman Fever"
    Edith Wharton
"The New Dress"
    Virginia Woolf
"A & P"
    John Updike
"Almos' a Man"
    Richard Wright

Name_____

Date _____

Short Story Analysis

Title of Short Story_____

_____

Author _____

_____

Setting _____

_____

_____

Characters _____

_____

_____

_____

Plot _____

_____

_____

_____

_____

_____

Theme _____

_____

_____

_____

_____

Point of View _____

_____

Style _____

_____

_____

Tone _____

_____

_____

Irony _____

_____

Symbolism _____

_____

_____

_____

Lesson 5
Writing the Analytical Paper

Objective

- To show students how to write a composition analyzing a short story

Notes to the Teacher

Advanced Placement students are assumed to know how to write a well-developed and unified paragraph based on a suitable topic sentence. This lesson continues work with the thesis sentence by reviewing the process of composition. Most important is the development of a single idea throughout the composition, through logical interconnections between paragraphs and thesis. Writing a composition that is an organic whole is difficult for most Advanced Placement students to achieve; the process is the discovery of how a single idea can unfold. The teaching strategy used here is the analytical sentence outline, which shows how each topic sentence is logically related to the thesis.

Students need feedback on their writing. This lesson can provide feedback in three ways: first, class discussion of students' theses and/or sentence outlines; second, your feedback during a class session given over to a writing laboratory when students are free to ask for comments before their writing is finished; third, peer critiquing of finished compositions, during which small groups are formed for the purpose of reading their themes to each other for reactions and suggestions for revisions. Peer critiquing can also be done on an individual basis, where each student makes a written critique of another student's paper.

Procedure

1. List on the board the following goal: Work out an easily discernible organizational pattern by which the topic sentence of each paragraph is logically related to the thesis.

2. Distribute **Handout 5** and **Handout 6**. Assign the working through of the handouts as they apply to "The Japanese Quince" for the next day. Students may work in pairs.

3. Assign students the task of producing analytical sentence outlines for papers they will write on a short story. You may wish to have the class critique these outlines by having students write their outlines on the board or by duplicating them.

   Discuss the idea of paragraph blocks with students. Inform them that a paragraph block is a block of paragraphs supporting the same detail. Tell them that the amount of information to be conveyed in each block, and its depth, determines the number of paragraphs needed in each block. Stress the lack of restrictions which accompanies paragraph blocks.

4. Have students examine the model theme on **Handout 7**.

5. Assign the writing of a composition on a short story. Depending upon the analytical skill of your class, you may decide to have all students write on the same story so that insights can be shared in class discussion after the papers are written, or you may assign a composition to be written on a story selected independently by each student.

Analytical Sentence Outline

This sheet suggests a process that results in an analytical sentence outline for a composition. This type of outline requires very close interlocking between thesis and topic sentences of paragraphs:

1. The central idea of the composition is the grammatical subject of the thesis sentence.

2. The topics in the predicate of the thesis sentence become the subjects of the topic sentences for the paragraphs of the composition.

3. The predicates of the topic sentences in the paragraphs are clearly and logically related to the central idea.[1]

The writing of a workable thesis for an analytical sentence outline is the result of a long and careful process.

Step 1— Focus on a topic, either assigned or chosen. You might want to base your analytical topics on one of the literary topics previously studied or on a personal reaction to a character or idea presented in the story.

Step 2— Carefully note from the story text every detail that might have relevance to your topic. Particularly note repetitions.

Step 3— Going back over your list of details, develop three or four general categories that will cover most of the details you have selected. These categories are your paragraph topics. Label (by initial letter of each topic) each detail according to the category into which it fits. Cross off those items that do not fit into a category.

Step 4— Arrange your topics (categories) in the order in which they should appear in your composition.

Step 5— List all of the details in topic 1. Develop a topic sentence for these details. Repeat for your other topics.

Step 6— Develop a thesis sentence that contains the central idea as the subject and delineates the topics of each paragraph in the predicate.

Step 7— Make sure that the predicates of each topic sentence for all paragraph blocks are clearly related to the central idea. There will be a lot of working back and forth between topic sentences and thesis during steps 5–7; the order of these steps is merely approximate.

[1] Edgar V. Roberts, *Writing Themes about Literature* (Englewood Cliffs, N.J.: Prentice Hall, 1977), 12.

Applying This Process to "The Japanese Quince"

Step 1— Topic—symbolism in "The Japanese Quince"

Steps 2 and 3— Details related to symbolism in the story, classified as R (rigidity), P (potential), T (twin). Repetitions are italicized after their first appearance.

P	sweetish sensation	P/T	also *smiling at the little tree*
P/R	feeling of emptiness just under fifth rib	R	Being married, they had not yet had occasion to speak.
R	thermometer stood at sixty	T	about Mr. Nilson's own height
P	a little tree had come out in blossom	T	*firm, well-colored cheeks*
T	firm, well-colored cheeks	T	*neat, brown mustache*
T	neat, brown mustaches	T	*round, well-opened, clear grey eyes*
T	round, well-opened, clear grey eyes	R/T	*black frock coat*
T/R	black frock coat	R/T	*morning paper clasped behind him*
T/R	morning paper laid out on sideboard	R/T	"Can you give me the name of that *tree*?"
P	queer *feeling*	R/T	"I was about to ask you that"
T	scrolled iron steps	R	first to see the little label
R	half an hour to breakfast	P	"Quite a *feelin'* in the air today."
R	circular path	R	"These exotics, they don't bear fruit."
T/R	*morning paper* clasped behind him	P	"*Pretty blossoms.*"
R	made two revolutions	P	"Nice fellow . . . I rather like him."
P	*feeling* had increased	R/T	*clasping* their *journals to their backs*
P	*sweetish* liquor in course within him	R	*scrolled iron steps*
P	faint aching just above his heart	P	spring sunlight darting and quivering into it
P	blackbird burst into song	P	*blackbird* chanting his heart out
P	this *tree* . . . covered with young blossoms	P	*queer sensation*, that choky *feeling* in his throat
P	little bright green leaves both round and spikey	P/T	also looking . . . at the little quince *tree*
P	smiling at the *tree*	R/T	*morning paper*
T	man with his *hands behind him*		

Step 4— Order is basically chronological:

    1. rigidity—situation when story opens

    2. potential—new possibility presented

    3. twin—reason new possibility is rejected

Step 5— Mr. Nilson's regimentation is signaled by

    1. paper in place

    2. breakfast always at 8:30

  * 3. circular path/two revolutions on walk

    4. never has spoken to his neighbor of five years

    5. reaction to tree is to look at label

  * 6. black frock coat

  * 7. name is Mr. Nilson

Symbols are marked with *; symbols reinforce characterization of other details.

Topic Sentence— Galsworthy carefully builds the impression that Mr. Nilson's life is empty, a rigid, sterile conformity, all of which is symbolized by his name.

Steps 6 and 7 result in the analytical sentence outline in **Handout 6.**

Name_____

Date _____

Diagram of an Analytical Composition

Introduction concludes with thesis stating central idea—symbolism

Galsworthy's use of symbolism, especially the technique of the double or mirror image, functions to define the restrictive lifestyle of Mr. Nilson, to illuminate the exciting potentiality of a new life, and to explain Mr. Nilson's retreat from rebirth.

Three infinitive phrases in predicate lead to topic sentences in developmental paragraph blocks.

Topic sentence for developmental paragraph block one

1. Galsworthy carefully builds the impression that Mr. Nilson's life is empty, a rigid, sterile conformity, all of which is symbolized by his name.

Predicate of topic sentence relates directly to symbolism.

Topic sentence for developmental paragraph block two

2. Through nature symbolism, Galsworthy introduces the possibility that Mr. Nilson can escape his rigid routine and claim a fresh, spontaneous life.

Complete predicate of topic sentence includes introductory adverbial prepositional phrase relating directly to symbolism.

Topic sentence for developmental paragraph block three

3. This very similarity between the two men leads to Mr. Nilson's judgment of his neighbor and is what keeps Mr. Nilson from breaking out of his sterile lifestyle, mirrored in his symbolic relationship to his double.

Predicate of topic sentence relates directly to symbolism.

Conclusion restates thesis idea

The loveliness of the Japanese quince and the vitality of the bird are rich symbols of the quality of life missed by the two men, wanting to be unique but caught in lives of repetitious conventionality, effectively expressed by the symbol of the double.

Symbolism in "The Japanese Quince:" A Model Composition

Although very little exterior action occurs in John Galsworthy's very short, short story, "The Japanese Quince," the perceptive reader knows that an opportunity has been passed by and that the protagonist has chosen to stay closed to the beauty of life rather than risk change. Some readers may not understand this "action," that consists entirely of not choosing and not responding; indeed, the protagonist himself is "unaccountably upset" at the end of the story, completely unaware of the choice he has made. Yet the author has, through subtle symbolism, made it clear to his readers. Galsworthy's use of symbolism, especially the technique of the double or mirror image, functions to define the restrictive lifestyle of Mr. Nilson, to illuminate the exciting potentiality of a new life, and to explain Mr. Nilson's retreat from rebirth.

Galsworthy carefully builds the impression that Mr. Nilson's life is an empty, rigid, sterile conformity, all of which is summarized by his name. Nilson, literally "the son of nothing," may have wealth (he has a dressing room and, presumably, a servant to lay out his morning paper on the sideboard) and reputation (he is "well known in the City"), but through his name Galsworthy signals that these are worthless. Mr. Nilson's life is best described by the symbol of a circle, like the circular path in the gardens upon which he makes two revolutions before he stops. His breakfast is always at 8:30; he always reads his journal. He wears his formal, black frock coat to the office every day. He has been so caught in the routine of his married life that his neighbor of five years is a "stranger," since "They had not yet had occasion to speak to one another."

However, through nature symbolism Galsworthy introduces the possibility that Mr. Nilson can escape his rigid routine and claim a fresh, spontaneous new life. It is spring fever that poor Mr. Nilson cannot recognize in himself when he is surprised to feel a "queer sensation," which he quickly locates "under his fifth rib" in an attempt to gain control of it. This sensation is both a judgment on Nilson's life (it is a "feeling of emptiness" and a "faint aching just above his heart") and an exciting potentiality (it is described twice as "sweet" and then connected to the "sweet lemony scent" of the Japanese quince.)

The Japanese quince, itself, is, the two neighbors agree, an "exotic," which "bears no fruit" but is "more alive than a tree." Although they "bear fruit" in terms of material wealth, the two men are less alive than the tree. The tree is covered with new blossoms and "little bright green leaves," a miracle of spring time, so full of new life and beauty that even the fuddy-duddy bankers smile at it and one another. After his neighbor remarks that he likes the sound of the blackbird, which has burst into song in the heart of the tree, Mr. Nilson thinks, "Nice fellow . . . I rather like him." The blackbird's somber appearance recalls the black frock coats of the two men and suggests that they, too, may, in their own banker-way, "burst into song."

But this very similarity between the two men leads to Mr. Nilson's judgment of his neighbor and is what keeps him from breaking out of his sterile lifestyle, mirrored in his symbolic relationship to his double. Since Mr. Nilson wants to be unique in his appreciation of the beauty of the little tree, he is "rather taken aback" when he sees his neighbor respond as he had. Galsworthy has explicitly doubled a long list of descriptive features of the two men so that the reader cannot miss the fact that the two men are mirror images of each other. About the same height, they both have "firm, well-colored cheeks, neat brown mustaches, and round, well-opened, clear grey eyes," as well as black frock coats and morning papers clasped behind their backs. Mr. Nilson's first words to his neighbor, "Can you give me the name of that tree?" are just what Mr. Tandram was going to say. The doubling of

Mr. Nilson in Mr. Tandram (as well as Mr. Tandram's name, which implies both humdrum and tandem) suggests that the protagonist is caught in a mold of conformity. But, since Mr. Nilson wants to be unique, ironically, it is just because his neighbor, too, appreciates the tree and the bird that he cannot allow himself to respond to them fully for fear of looking foolish as he judges Mr. Tandram to be. The technique of the double, then, serves two purposes: to indicate the mold of conformity in which Mr. Nilson exists and to keep Mr. Nilson from breaking out of that mold.

Galsworthy has implied a great deal in this brief story. The loveliness of the Japanese quince and the vitality of the bird are rich symbols of the quality of life missed by the two men, wanting to be unique but caught in lives of repetitious conventionality, effectively expressed by the symbol of the double.

Lesson 6
Introducing Poems

Objective

- To enable students to approach poems comfortably and confidently

Notes to the Teacher

Even on the Advanced Placement level, students are sometimes fearful or reluctant about the study of poetry. A major hurdle is mastered when they realize that they can comprehend and appreciate poems. It is helpful to point out that they need not be frustrated by difficulties in assessing a poem's total purpose or effect after the first few readings of it and that with determination, understanding of a poem may grow.

In this lesson, students meet four poems from the American literary tradition. The approach is open-ended, and the goals are understanding and enjoyment.

Procedure

1. Point out to the students that a good way to begin a study of poetry is simply to read and respond to poems.

2. Have students silently read "A Noiseless Patient Spider" on **Handout 8**. Then have a volunteer read it aloud.

3. Ask students the following questions:
   a. What is the first stanza about?

   The speaker is watching the spider cast out filaments of web.

   b. What happens in the second stanza?

   There is a comparison made between the speaker and the spider. The speaker's mind is constantly casting out filaments of thought, trying to make connections that will last.

   c. What do the spider and the speaker have in common?

   Both are isolated, surrounded by space, constantly and patiently trying to make necessary connections.

4. Point out that the speaker's situation here is one we can all identify with—a quiet, solitary moment filled with intellectual energy in a search for meaningful connections. Ask students to reread the poem and recall their own experiences that the poem brings to mind. Have volunteers share their experiences.

5. Have students read the other three poems on **Handout 8**. Then have volunteers read them aloud.

6. Have each student select one of the three and probe it to discover

   a. What is its main concern?

   b. What feelings, attitudes, and insights are expressed?

   c. How can the poem be related to our lives and experiences?

7. Discuss each of the poems by having students share their insights. You may want to begin with the one chosen by the most students. If one of the poems was not selected by anyone, take time to look at it with the whole class.

Suggested Responses:

"After Great Pain, a Formal Feeling Comes"
a. *The speaker describes the half-dead, stunned, remote feeling that comes after a person has been terribly hurt.*
b. *The poem has a quiet but heavy feeling, like the experience it describes. It reflects the immobilizing effect of painful experiences. The last stanza indicates that this "Hour of Lead" is a critical moment. The person may not recover.*
c. *Students have undoubtedly experienced and seen others experience the blankness that can follow personal disaster.*

"Those Winter Sundays"
a. *The speaker describes a childhood experience from the adult point of view. The care of the speaker's father is evident,*

but the child lacked the gratitude and insight the adult speaker now has.

b. There is nostalgia in the speaker's awareness of the father's love. There is realization of the childish way of taking things for granted.

c. The poem evokes a desire to appreciate people, especially parents, while we have them with us—not to miss the love they expressed by performing ordinary, glamourless duties.

"The Bean Eaters"

a. The poem describes two old people living extremely simply in a rented room, surrounded by various things that recall both happy and regrettable past events.

b. The "twinklings and twinges" in the last stanza bring us close to these old people, who may "have lived their day," but are certainly not dead yet. The speaker's attitude moves from cool objectivity in the first line to personal warmth in the images in the last few lines.

c. Students may relate the poem to old people they have known or seen.

Name_____

Date _____

Four Poems

A Noiseless Patient Spider

A noiseless patient spider,
I mark'd where on a little promontory it stood isolated,
Mark'd how to explore the vacant vast surrounding,
It launch'd forth filament, filament, filament, out of itself,
Ever unreeling them, ever tirelessly speeding them.
And you, O my soul, where you stand,
Surrounded, detached, in measureless oceans of space,
Ceaselessly musing, venturing, throwing, seeking the spheres
to connect them,
Till the bridge you will need be form'd, till the ductile anchor
hold,
Till the gossamer thread you fling catch somewhere, Oh my soul.

—*Walt Whitman*

After Great Pain, a Formal Feeling Comes

After great pain, a formal feeling comes—
The nerves sit ceremonious, like Tombs—
The still Heart questions was it He, that bore,
And Yesterday, or Centuries before?

The Feet, mechanical, go round—
Of Ground, or Air, or Ought—
A Wooden way
Regardless grown,
A Quartz contentment, like a stone—

This is the Hour of Lead—
Remembered, if outlived,
As Freezing persons, recollect the Snow—
First—Chill—then Stupor—then the letting go—

—*Emily Dickinson*

Name_____

Date _____

Those Winter Sundays

Sundays too my father got up early
and put his clothes on in the blueblack cold,
then with cracked hands that ached
from labor in the weekday weather made
banked fires blaze. No one ever thanked him.

I'd wake and hear the cold splintering, breaking.
When the rooms were warm, he'd call,
and slowly I would rise and dress,
fearing the chronic angers of that house,

Speaking indifferently to him,
who had driven out the cold
and polished my good shoes as well.
What did I know, what did I know
of love's austere and lonely offices?

—*Robert Hayden*

The Bean Eaters

They eat beans mostly, this old yellow pair.
Dinner is a casual affair.
Plain chipware on a plain and creaking wood,
Tin flatware.
Two who are Mostly Good.
Two who have lived their day,
But keep on putting on their clothes
And putting things away.
And remembering . . .
Remembering, with twinklings and twinges,
As they lean over the beans in their rented back room
    that is full of beads and receipts and dolls and clothes,
    tobacco crumbs, vases and fringes.

—*Gwendolyn Brooks*

Lesson 7
Identifying Tools of Analysis

Objectives

- To equip students with necessary poetic terminology
- To illustrate this terminology using poems previously studied

Notes to the Teacher

The terms included here are intended as a review. Time allowed on the discussion of the handout will vary according to students' need and familiarity with terms.

Procedure

1. Distribute **Handout 9**.

2. Review poetic terms.

3. Identify and discuss the suggested examples of each term, as found in the poems in **Handout 8**.

   Examples of poetic terms:
   Denotation—Have students check the dictionary meaning of these words taken from the poems:

austere	gossamer
chronic	promontory
ductile	

   Connotation—"Two who have lived their day," implies that the people are near the end of their lives.
   Imagery—"...hear the cold..." (sense of sound)
   "They eat beans mostly..." (sense of taste)
   "...cracked hands that ached..." (sense of touch)
   Simile—"...nerves sit ceremonious, like Tombs—"
   "A Quartz contentment, like a stone—"
   (comparisons using *like* or *as*)

   Metaphor—"This is the Hour of Lead—" (comparison of unlike objects)
   Personification—"The stiff Heart questions..." (gives heart a human function)
   "...O my soul, where you stand," (gives anatomy to the soul)
   "...nerves sit..." (gives human function)
   Rhythm/Meter—"The Feet, mechanical, go round—
   Of Ground, or Air, or Ought—" (iambic tetrameter, trimeter)
   Rime—"...this old yellow pair.
   Dinner is a casual affair." ("pair"/ "affair")
   Alliteration—"...with twinklings and twinges," (repetition of beginning *tw* sound)
   Assonance—"...beads and receipts..." (repetition of long E sound)
   Consonance—"...clothes on in the blueblack cold," (repetition of K sound)
   Allusion—"...was it He..." (reference to Christ)
   Paradox—"...love's austere and lonely offices?" (We do not usually think of love in these terms.)
   Form—"Those Winter Sundays" has fourteen lines, as do most sonnets. Notice the indented final lines of "The Bean Eaters," which set apart the treasures of the old couple.

4. Ask students to write theme statements for each of the poems. These theme statements could be the bases for critical papers.

   Suggestions:
   a. In "After Great Pain, a Formal Feeling Comes," Emily Dickinson illustrates the suffering that follows personal loss.

b. Walt Whitman's "A Noiseless Patient Spider" encourages humankind to reach out to one another to form lasting relationships.

c. Gwendolyn Brooks speaks of the remnants of long life that have only personal value in her poem, "The Bean Eaters."

d. Taking for granted the love and acts of love of a parent, Robert Hayden acknowledges he was unaware of the duties love entails in his poem, "Those Winter Sundays."

Name_____

Date _____

Poetic Terminology

Denotation—the exact, dictionary meaning of a particular word

Connotation—emotional word associations usually based on individual experience, regional experience, or universal implications

Imagery—words that arouse the sense of sight, sound, smell, taste, or touch

Simile—generally introduced by *like* or *as*, a comparison of two dissimilar objects

Metaphor—a comparison of two dissimilar objects, without using *like* or *as*; endowing the first object with the qualities of the second object

Personification—the application of human characteristic to animals, inanimate objects, or ideas

Rhythm/Meter—the regularity of recurrence, which establishes a repetitive pattern of stressed and unstressed syllables

Rime—the repetition of all sounds, beginning with the accented vowel, in two or more words

Alliteration—the repetition of initial consonant sounds

Assonance—the repetition of vowel sounds within a line of poetry

Consonance—the repetition of consonant sounds within a line of poetry

Allusion—reference to a well-known historical or literary figure or event

Paradox—an apparent contradiction that actually may contain a universal truth

Form—the structure or organization of the work that gives it unity, through arrangement, rime scheme, number of lines, etc. Different forms of poetry include haiku, sonnet, ode, elegy, lyric, epic, and many others.

Thesis Statement—a general statement of a major aspect of the literary work that can be substantiated through analysis of elements

Lesson 8
Unlocking a Poem

Objective

- To enable students to use their understanding of literary elements as a key to opening up the meaning of an individual poem

Notes to the Teacher

The compressed use of language in poems sometimes makes them appear to be difficult. When encountering these works, students need to be able to use their understanding of literary elements as analytical keys. There is, of course, no sure-fire method of grasping all poems. In this lesson, students use Wallace Stevens's "Autumn Refrain" in a guided analysis.

Procedure

1. Tell students that this lesson will focus on developing their abilities to read and analyze poems as preparation for group projects and individual compositions.

2. Have students silently read "Autumn Refrain" on **Handout 10**. Ask them to re-read it several times, and then have a volunteer read it aloud.

3. Point out that **Handouts 1** and **9** summarize literary devices to be aware of in approaching any literary work. The challenge is to become sensitive to which devices can be helpful in understanding a specific literary work.

4. Ask students to complete part A of **Handout 10**.

   Suggested Responses:

   1. *Autumn carries multiple connotations, including both celebration of the harvest and melancholy at the end of another yearly cycle. Refrain is a musical term denoting a regularly repeated series of words and melody.*

   2. *Divisions occur midway through l.3, part way through l.7, and at the end of l.12. The first unit points out that the concerns of day and dusk are "gone." The second focuses on the harvest moon and the*

   nightingale. The third modifies the first, noting that some of the concerns of day are, after all, still quietly present. The fourth unit points out the melancholy that pervades the stillness of the night.

   3. *While there is more than one way to approach this poem, imagery and paradox are dominant elements in it and thus are probably the most helpful tools.*

5. Ask students to underline all images in the poem and to use lines to link similar images.

   Example: "skreak and skritter" in l.1 is echoed in "skreaking and skrittering" in l.10. The yellow moon and the nightingale are also key images. Also note recurring use of musical terms, including "refrain" in the title, "measureless measures" in l.5, "nameless air" in l.6, and "key" in ll.13–14.

6. Ask students to circle the paradoxes.

   Suggested Responses:

   "measureless measures," "name of a nameless air," "beneath the stillness ... some skreaking and skrittering residuum."

7. Ask students to answer the questions on **Handout 10**, part B.

   Suggested Responses:

   1. *A person in or near a forest at the very beginning of an autumn night*

   2. *The speaker hears nothing but has a sense of a "residuum" of daytime sounds. The speaker sees nothing in the darkness except the yellow moon and, probably, silhouettes.*

   3. *Desolation, loneliness, melancholy*

   4. *The poem is about an autumn night. The refrain is the uneasy silence and emptiness mentioned throughout the poem.*

   5. *To communicate the eerie, restless stillness of an autumn night*

   6. *Example—In "Autumn Refrain," Wallace Stevens uses sound imagery to accentuate the eerie quietness of an autumn night.*

Autumn Refrain

The skreak and skritter of evening gone
And grackles gone and sorrows of the sun,
The sorrows of sun, too, gone . . . the moon and moon,
The yellow moon of words about the nightingale
In measureless measures, not a bird for me
But the name of a bird and the name of a nameless air
I have never—shall never hear. And yet beneath
The stillness of everything gone, and being still,
Being and sitting still, something resides,
Some skreaking and skrittering residuum,
And grates these evasions of the nightingale
Though I have never—shall never hear that bird.
And the stillness is in the key, all of it is,
The stillness is all in the key of that desolate sound.

—*Wallace Stevens*

Part A.
Preliminary Considerations

1. What might the title of this poem imply?

2. Use slash marks to divide the poem into units of meaning. Describe the content of each unit.

3. Identify literary devices that are important in this poem and that might help in getting to the heart of it.

Part B.

1. Who is the speaker in this poem? Describe the time and place setting.

2. What can the speaker hear? See?

3. What is the speaker's mood?

4. What does the title have to do with the poem as a whole?

5. What seems to be the purpose of "Autumn Refrain?"

6. If you were to write a critical essay about this poem, what might your thesis be?

Lesson 9
Experiencing the Analytic Process

Objectives

- To have students successfully identify correct answers to questions relating to a particular poem
- To have students formulate thesis statements about this poem
- To have students relate personal experience with loss of identify to Auden's "The Unknown Citizen"

Notes to the Teacher

Auden's "The Unknown Citizen" is an attack on the loss of identity people inevitably suffer through the advancement of technology. In this lesson, you have the opportunity to explore this loss with your students.

Procedure

1. Distribute 3 × 5 cards, and ask students to write their telephone numbers in large print on one side. Use pins to attach these cards to the front of their clothing. During the following lessons, students may refer to each other by these numbers.

2. Distribute copies of **Handouts 11** and **12**. Allow time for completion.

3. Ask volunteers to discuss the support found in the poem for each answer.

   Suggested Responses:

1. b	6. d
2. d	7. d
3. a	8. b
4. b	9. a
5. d	10. d

4. Ask students to write individual thesis statements for Auden's poem.

5. Call students by numbers to write their statements on the board. Discuss differences and similarities.

Suggested Responses:

1. *In "The Unknown Citizen," W.H. Auden illustrates how government can de-personalize our identities.*

2. *Our individuality is forfeited when we conform to governmental standards, says W.H. Auden in his poem, "The Unknown Citizen.*

3. *The workings of bureaucracy extract a terrible price, according to W.H. Auden's "The Unknown Citizen."*

Optional Activities

1. Ask students to write their reactions to this use of numbers as identification, giving other examples where they are known only by number (e.g., library check-out).

2. Make a list of all the governmental agencies Auden uses, and find their counterparts in the governmental agencies of this country.

Name_____

Date _____

The Unknown Citizen

JS/07/M/378
THIS MARBLE MONUMENT IS ERECTED BY THE STATE
He was found by the Bureau of Statistics to be
One against whom there was no official complaint,
And all the reports on his conduct agree
That, in the modern sense of an old-fashioned word, he was a saint,
For in everything he did he served the Great Community,
Except for the war till the day he retired
He worked in the factory and never got fired,
But satisfied his employers, Fudge Motors Inc.
Yet he wasn't a scab or odd in his views,
For his Union reports that he paid his dues,
(Our report on his Union shows it was sound)
And our Social Psychology workers found
That he was popular with his mates and liked a drink.
The Press are convinced that he bought a paper every day
And that his reactions to poetry were normal in every way.
Policies taken out in his name prove that he was fully insured,
And his Health Card shows he was once in hospital but left it cured.
Both Producers Research and High-Grade Living declare
He was fully sensible to the advantages of the Installment Plan
And had everything necessary to the Modern Man,
A gramophone, a radio, a car, and a Frigidaire.
Our researchers into public opinion are content
That he held the proper opinions for the time of year
When there was peace, he was for peace; where there was war, he went.
He was married and added five children to the population,
Which our Eugenists say was the right number for a parent of his generation.
And our teachers report that he never interfered with their education.
Was he free? Was he happy? The question is absurd:
Had anything been wrong, we certainly should have heard.

—W. H. Auden

Name_____

Date _____

W. H. Auden
"The Unknown Citizen"

Circle the letter of the correct answer.

1. The subject of this poem is
   a. a retired civil servant
   b. an ordinary person
   c. a poet
   d. a deprived individual

2. The subject's childhood
   a. was gloriously happy
   b. was miserable
   c. influenced the adult he became
   d. is not mentioned

3. The speaker in this poem is
   a. a government official
   b. the citizen himself
   c. a military leader
   d. a computer programmer

4. The title means
   a. the citizen died nobly in a war
   b. government has robbed the citizen of his identity
   c. all citizens are referred to by number
   d. the state wishes to honor a famous citizen

5. The question of "free" and "happy" is considered absurd because
   a. conformity insures happiness and freedom
   b. it is better to conform
   c. the question is irrelevant
   d. the question lacks sufficient data

6. Auden is attacking
   a. the spineless citizen
   b. the causes of war
   c. man's indifference
   d. government that reduces people to objects

7. Auden is praising
   a. individuality
   b. our society
   c. the citizen's ability to understand poetry
   d. nothing

8. Government considers the citizen "a saint" because
   a. he performed miracles
   b. he did not resist conformity
   c. he was a union member
   d. he was free and happy

9. Auden makes us aware
   a. of the all-consuming power of government
   b. that duty is its own reward
   c. that happiness is within the reach of all
   d. that to defy authority is foolish

10. The "marble monument" suggests
    a. great fame
    b. eternity
    c. imprisonment
    d. death

Lesson 10
Poem Analysis by a Group

Objective

- To give students practice in poem analysis by working in pairs on a self-selected poem

Notes to the Teacher

Although students should be able to do a line-by-line paraphrase of the poem they analyze, you may want to warn them that a paraphrase of a poem instead of an analysis is no more adequate than a plot summary of a story. A list of suggested poems for analysis is included on page 46.

Procedure

1. Distribute **Handouts 13** and **14**. Have students use the worksheet to analyze Shakespeare's "Sonnet 146." Share responses.

   Suggested Responses:

   1. One should starve the body to feed the soul.

   2. Speaker—the poet, a mortal who confesses his materialism

   To whom—the poet's own soul

   Conflict—the desires of the body vs. the health of the soul

   Catalyst—the spending of money on adornments for the body

   3. Signal word—Then, line 9

   Part A—lines 1 to 8;

   Function—rhetorical questions press the need for conversion: why spend so much money on the body since it will soon die?

   Part B—lines 9 to 14

   Function—exhortations to ascetism so the soul can gain immortality

   Key line—line 9, advising the soul to deny the body

   4. Tone—insistent, solemn, moralistic

   Paradox—soul is fed by not feeding the body

   Death slays the body but is slain by the soul which gains immortality: "Death once dead"

   6. Contrasts—body is rich, soul is poor; inverted to soul is rich, body is poor

   7. Metaphors—body=house; "thy fading mansion," "painting thy outward walls," "so short a lease"

   Feeding—begins literally with worms feeding on body; then metaphorically, soul feeds on Death (gains immortality through death) who "feeds on me" (again, Death literally eats my body via worms)

   Slave=soul; master=body in octave because soul gives body what it wants; changes in sestet to body is servant to the soul because soul denies body for good of the soul

2. Have pairs of students select a poem that appeals to them. Students should use **Handout 13** as a tool to enlarge their understandings of their poems. You may wish to collect the work sheets to gauge student progress.

45

Poem Suggestions for Analysis

These poems were selected from the many workable ones on the basis of complexity, range of difficulty, and length. Each poem below is complex enough to yield a full paper. The poems have been arranged according to two levels of difficulty so the better students may choose more challenging poems if they desire. The beginning list of sonnets has been included because their brevity and structure invite detailed analysis. Poems that have appeared on previous Advanced Placement tests are indicated by an asterisk (*).

Sonnets _____

"That Night When Joy Began"
  W. H. Auden

"Batter My Heart, Three Personed God"
  John Donne

* "Since There's No Help"
  Michael Drayton

"God's Grandeur"
  Gerard Manley Hopkins

"The Caged Skylark"
  Gerard Manley Hopkins

"On His Blindness"
  John Milton

"Anthem for Doomed Youth"
  Wilfred Owen

"No Longer Mourn for Me"
  William Shakespeare

"That Time of Year"
  William Shakespeare

"Lines Composed upon Westminster Bridge"
  William Wordsworth

Poems of Average Difficulty _____

"Dover Beach"
  Matthew Arnold

* "Musee des Beaux Arts"
  W. H. Auden

* "One Art"
  Elizabeth Bishop

"The Lifeguard"
  James Dickey

* "The last night that she lived"
  Emily Dickinson

"The Good Morrow"
  John Donne

* "Choose Something Like a Star"
  Robert Frost

* "Design"
  Robert Frost

* "The Most of It"
  Robert Frost

* "For Jane Meyers"
  Louise Gluck

"Channel Firing"
  Thomas Hardy

"To an Athlete, Dying Young"
  A. E. Housman

"Losses"
  Randall Jarrell

* "Bright Star"
  John Keats

"Patterns"
  Amy Lowell

"Water"
  Robert Lowell

"Dr. Sigmund Freud Discovers the Sea Shell"
  Archibald MacLeish

"The Horses"
  Edwin Muir

"Love Poem"
  John Frederick Nims

"Parting, without a Sequel"
  John Crowe Ransom

* "Storm Warnings"
  Adrienne Rich

"Aaron Stark"
  Edwin Arlington Robinson

"The Right Things Happen to the Happy Man"
  Theodore Roethke

"Ulysses"
  Alfred Lord Tennyson

"Do Not Go Gentle into That Good Night"
  Dylan Thomas

* "Spring and All"
  William Carlos Williams

* "There Was a Boy"
  William Wordsworth

More Difficult Poems _____

* "As I Walked Out One Evening"
  W. H. Auden

* "Law Like Love"
  W. H. Auden

* "O gun"
  E. K. Braithwaite

"My Last Duchess"
  Robert Browning

"anyone lived in a pretty how town"
  e. e. cummings

"Valediction: Forbidding Mourning"
  John Donne

* "The Groundhog"
  Richard Eberhart

"Love Song of J. Alfred Prufrock"
  T. S. Eliot

"The Hollow Men"
  T. S. Eliot

* "Directive"
  Robert Frost

* "The Collar"
  George Herbert

"The Windhover"
  Gerard Manley Hopkins

"Eighth Air Force"
  Randall Jarrell

"I Hear an Army"
  James Joyce

"Ode on a Grecian Urn"
  John Keats

* "Poetry of Departures"
  Philip Larkin

"Mushrooms"
  Sylvia Plath

* "Sow"
  Sylvia Plath

"Peter Quince at the Clavier"
  Wallace Stevens

* "The Great Scarf of Birds"
  John Updike

* "Wild Swans at Coole"
  W. B. Yeats

Name_____

Date _____

Poetry Worksheet

Use this worksheet as a tool in independently analyzing a poem. Remember that not all elements apply to every poem.

Title of Poem _____

Author _____

1. Sentence paraphrase

2. Dramatic situation

    Speaker _____

    To whom _____

    Setting _____

    Occasion _____

    Conflict _____

    Catalyst _____

3. Thought structure

    Transitional (signal) words _____

    Part A, lines _____ to _____

    Function: _____

    Part B, lines _____ to _____

    Function: _____

    Part C, lines _____ to _____

    Function: _____

    Part D, lines _____ to _____

    Function: _____
    (Add parts, as needed, on back)

    Key line _____

Name_____

Date _____

4. Emotional structure _____

   Change _____

   Tone _____

   Loaded words or images _____

   Heavy connotations _____

   Irony/paradox _____

5. Title _____

   Synonyms (or related words) _____

   Significance _____

6. Contrasts or parallels _____

7. Figurative language—metaphors, similes, personification _____

8. Best adaptation of sound to sense _____

Name_____

Date _____

Sonnet 146

Poor soul, the center of my sinful earth,
Thrall to these rebel powers that thee array,
Why dost thou pine within and suffer dearth,
Painting thy outward walls so costly gay?
Why so large cost, having so short lease,
Dost thou upon thy fading mansion spend?
Shall worms, inheritors of this excess,
Eat up thy charge? Is this thy body's end?
Then, soul, live thou upon thy servant's loss,
And let that pine to aggravate thy store;
Buy terms divine in selling hours of dross;
Within be fed, without be rich no more:
    So shall thou feed on Death, that feeds on men,
    And Death once dead, there's no more dying then.

—William Shakespeare

Lesson 11
Developing an Analytical Paper

Objective

• To enable students to develop supporting evidence for an analytical paper on a poem

Notes to the Teacher

The beginning student of literature may argue for the relativity of taste and response—that any response to a literary work is valid as long as it is felt by the reader. Though this view held by critic Louise Rosenblatt is now in favor with some English teachers, the approach of this material and of the Advanced Placement testing program is that an interpretation of a literary work is only as strong as the evidence from the work that is cited to support it. On the other hand, the Advanced Placement teacher must be very careful not to assume one correct interpretation, but to be open to new insights based on fresh evidence.

Basic to the process of supporting ideas with good evidence is a tight organizational structure with well-focused topic sentences, as explained in Lesson 5. When the topic sentence is not clearly focused, the evidence cannot be effective. This lesson, then, assumes Lesson 5 as background. Students should have completed **Handout 14** before beginning this lesson.

Procedure

1. Explain the use of the word *thesis* in university doctoral programs. It is the major idea of a long paper based on original research that must be defended by the author in an oral examination before a committee of five faculty members. Draw an analogy between the Ph.D. candidate's defense of his or her thesis and the student author's support of his or her thesis in a paper. For both, the quality of the supporting evidence determines the success or failure of the project.

2. Distribute **Handout 15**. After reviewing the explanation on the handout, play Cinderella Grab Bag. Cut up the evidence section of the handout pages, and put the slips into a box. Then have each student draw a slip, which he or she then must evaluate. The evaluation should be done as to the quality of evidence it represents for a composition on the story of Cinderella with the thesis written on the handout. Students may find each statement either

   a. strong evidence as it is

   b. needing another point or explanation to support it (in this case, students must provide the support)

   c. not usable as evidence

   After the game, you should summarize important points. Strong evidence needs no explanation in the composition. Evidence falling in (b) above must have the explanatory material to be valid. Material in category (c) should not appear on its own. If used, it should be subordinated grammatically to provide necessary context.

3. Have students read **Handout 16**. Help them understand comments on both compositions. Ask students to supply examples from the model composition for each of the three ways evidence may be used, such as

   a. What the author means—development paragraph two, explanation of conversion idea in sestet; development paragraph three, explanation of housing metaphor

   b. How author achieves meaning—development paragraph one, how idea of conversion is presented; development paragraph two, inversion of line three in line ten; development paragraph three, emphasis on "cost"

   c. Why author chooses this technique—development paragraph one, poetic inversion parallels religious conversion idea; development paragraph three, clothing metaphor is implied because it is trite

51

Name_____

Date _____

Cinderella Grab Bag

To play this game with skill (and to write a good composition), you must know the difference between strong and weak analytical evidence.

Strong Analytical Evidence is
    1—what the author means
    2—how the author achieves meaning
    3—why the author uses this technique

Strong Analytical Evidence is not
    1—what happens (plot summary)
    2—what the author says (paraphrase)

Sometimes the same fact may be strong evidence in one composition but not obviously relevant in a second composition with the same thesis. The difference lies in the way in which the fact is related (or not related) to the author's purpose. Each detail must be linked to a logical cause-effect chain leading to the author's purpose. Cinderella Grab Bag asks you to evaluate evidence for a composition on the well-known fairy tale.

Thesis for Cinderella Composition—In the well-known fairy tale, which has an easily understood morality, the character of Cinderella is good and pure, while her stepsisters are evil.

1 Cinderella sat by the fireside.	**6** Stepsisters cut their feet to fit the glass slipper.
2 Stepsisters had their eyes plucked out by birds.	**7** Cinderella did all the work uncomplainingly.
3 Cinderella had a fairy godmother.	**8** Stepsisters were their mother's favorites.
4 Stepsisters made fun of Cinderella for wanting to go to the ball.	**9** Cinderella was helped by the animals.
5 Cinderella was loved by the prince.	**10** Stepsisters were jealous of Cinderella's beauty.

11	Cinderella came home at midnight.

12	Stepsisters wore dark, vivid dresses to the ball.

13	Cinderella dropped her slipper.

14	Stepsisters were ugly.

15	Cinderella was beautiful.

16	Cinderella had tiny feet.

17	Cinderella came home with a pumpkin.

18	Cinderella was not treated fairly by her stepmother.

19	Cinderella was an orphan.

20	Cinderella wore white to the ball.

Analysis of Shakespeare's Sonnet 146

A Model Composition

Every student of English knows that Shakespeare was skilled at reworking old, worn-out plots into fabulous inventions in his plays. It is not surprising, then, to discover that he was also adept at making a hackneyed idea appear new and exciting in a sonnet. In "Sonnet 146," Shakespeare affirms the monastic idea that *discipline and denial of the body's desires strengthens the soul and gains immortality.* His rather conventional idea that one must starve the body to feed the soul takes on new life as he skillfully manipulates the poetic techniques of the *sonnet form— metaphors relating to materialism and the ironic techniques of paradox and inversion.*

The moralistic nature of the theme is served well by the sonnet form, modified in this poem to emphasize an octave of *rhetorical questions* followed by a sestet of *exhortations, both suggesting a religious conversion.* The heavy moralistic device of rhetorical questions followed by exhortation escapes preachiness because Shakespeare addresses them both to his own soul. Although the usual Shakespearean sonnet form of three quatrains and a couplet is still present, this sonnet also has a thought division occurring between the octave and the sestet. The first eight lines present *the need for conversion* through four rhetorical questions, all of which ask why the soul is spending so much money and effort to appease the material demands of the body, since it will soon die. *Signaled by a repetition* ("Poor soul" of line 1 becomes "Then soul" in line 9), the *exhortations to conversion* begin in the sestet. Now the poet urges his soul to neglect his body and mortify his flesh ("without be rich no more") so that his soul can gain eternal life ("there's no more dying then"). The idea of *conversion* is implicit in the sestet: after the sinful ways of the materialistic body ("my sinful earth") are enumerated in the octave, the soul must give them up for spiritual rewards in a complete turnabout, as the word conversion implies. The *shift to conversion is most tellingly seen by comparing lines 3 and 10,* which closely parallel each other. "Thou (soul) pine" becomes "that (body) pine" and "suffer death" becomes "aggravate thy store," so that the original meaning in line 3 is completely inverted—*a poetic inversion that parallels the religious experience of conversion.*

By economically developing the *metaphors of housing* and, to a lesser extent, *clothing, both types of materialistic desires,* Shakespeare clearly sets forth the dangers of paying attention to the *materialistic demands of the body at the expense of the soul.* The dominant metaphor in the poem is investment in a house; in the poem the house stands for the body, and its decoration indicates the adornment of the body. The soul is both the tenant of the house (the soul resides within the body) and the landlord who is refurbishing it by "painting thy outward walls so costly gay" (the soul makes the decisions about whether or not to decorate the body). The emphasis on the word "cost" by its repetition in lines 5 and 6 implies that the soul is paying too high a price for the body's materialism, i.e., that the pursuit of worldly goods results in the shriveling of the spirit. The house metaphor also includes a development of the idea of investment.

> Why so large cost, having so short a lease,
> Dost thou upon thy fading mansion spend? (lines 5 and 6)

With only three words, "lease" and "fading mansion," Shakespeare adds another dimension to the house metaphor: the idea that when a lease is about to expire, it is a foolish investment to spend money fixing up an old house. With the same economy of words, Shakespeare implies a whole new metaphor, that of clothing the body. Since this metaphor is not as fresh as the house figure (and clothing the body might also be taken literally), Shakespeare delicately touches it with only one word, "array": "Thrall to these revel powers that thee array" (line 2). Clothes are the only things that "array" a body, yet Shakespeare makes his reader find the clothes between the lines. The two metaphors of clothing and housing are brought together in two terms, "rich" (line 12) and "this excess" (line 7), *both of which pass judgment on the excesses of the body's materialism* and apply equally well to clothing and housing.

The *ironic idea* that a person gains eternal life for the soul by neglect of the body is masterfully worked out through the techniques of *paradox and inversion*. Feeding, a third *metaphor of materialism*, is introduced at the very end of the octave to show the fearful outcome of over-emphasis upon materialism for the body's sake:

> Shall worms, inheritors of this excess,
> Eat up thy charge? Is this thy body's end? (lines 7–8)

But Shakespeare uses the technique of ironic inversion to explain how the soul might escape this fate. Instead of allowing the body to be fattened for the worms, the soul should feed itself ("within be fed"). The concluding paradox pushes the feeding metaphor to extremity:

> So shall thou feed on Death, that feeds on men,
> And Death, once dead, there's no more dying then. (lines 13–14)

In this paradoxical couplet, Shakespeare sets out three terms, related by their successive cannibalism: the soul feeds on Death, which feeds on men. The paradox is that Death, the middle term of the three, is both eater and eaten, both slayer and slain. The crucial term that leads to an understanding of the paradox is the first one: how does the soul feed on Death? The whole sonnet provides the answer. By denying the body material pleasure, the soul is becoming purer and stronger. Living not for life on earth but for eternal life, i.e., Death, and thus both "feeding on Death," and killing Death, Death is no longer to be feared because "there's no more dying then." Thus is Death slain.

Shakespeare establishes *one more metaphorical relationship*, that of master to servant in the octave, which he then inverts in the sestet *to reenforce the conversion theme*. Initially, the soul was "thrall to those rebel powers" even though it is truly "center to my sinful earth" and should, therefore, be master of the body. Through the master-servant metaphor, Shakespeare summarizes the problem and the solution. The body and its material desires have wrongfully become dominant over the soul and its spiritual concerns. Only through *conversion, established through inversion of the metaphor* so that the former slave becomes master, can the proper relationship and the problem's solution be attained. In the sestet, the soul is exhorted to take charge and invert the relationship—to make the body not the slave or "thrall" like the soul in the octave, but the "servant." The choice of diction indicates a more harmonious and proper relationship than the former coercive master-slave relationship. This inversion, by which the soul becomes the master instead of the slave of the body, is the means by which the spirit will be nourished and immortality will be gained to overcome Death.

To convey a simple religious idea of asceticism, Shakespeare has worked out a dazzling array of poetic fireworks. Whether Shakespeare is effective as a preacher in converting sinful souls may be debated, but as a poet creating a jewel of a sonnet, he is an undisputed master.

A Student Composition

William Shakespeare, in "Sonnet 146," shows his attitude toward the importance of the body and soul. The form and diction of the poem, both, show that Shakespeare believed the soul is much more important than the body. One should not adorn the mortal body since its master is the immortal soul.

The form of the poem is question and answer: the question is "Why pay so much attention to your decaying body?" and the answer is "it is better to adorn your soul, for it will never die." Being a Shakespearean sonnet, the 4-4-4-2 form is not neglected, although in Italian sonnet form, the first eight lines contain the question and the last six yield the answer. The question is first stated as "Why dost thou (soul) pine within and suffer dearth (from neglect of attention), painting thy outward walls so costly gay?" *The question is repeated to make the answer—already obvious from the diction—more forceful.* The seventh and eighth lines add two more questions, to both of which the reader will answer "yes," *that show the eventual waste of not following the poet's advice*; worms are the final "inheritors" of the body. The soul, as explained metaphorically in the last six lines, will never die and thus defeats death. The address in the ninth line "Then, soul," is a repeat of the first line "Poor soul," and is present *because the poet is ready to give the answers to the questions he has posed*, indirectly, of course, to make the reader think and realize the truth, the sense the poet is making.

Through his choice of diction, Shakespeare stresses that the expenses of the body are unnecessary and deprive the soul. The "poor soul" must be "thrall to these rebel powers" that clothe the body with unneeded objects. By using "thrall" and "rebel," Shakespeare expresses the idea *that caring too much for the body enslaves one.* He calls the money spent on the body an "excess." The body is, after all, only *outward walls*; a *holder of rebel powers*; a *fading mansion*; and a *servant* to the soul. The last three lines make use of the metaphor of eating, used before in the poem with the worms, for Shakespeare's final statement. The soul should "feed on Death" and be feeding itself and not the body. "Death once dead" is a clinching paradox that the reader must chew next in order that he sees the immorality of the soul.

Shakespeare may not have a novel point of view when he elevates the status of the soul above the body. However, his genius allows him to illuminate the contradictions present in a life dominated by an inner struggle. His soul has, thus far, outlived his body.

Comments on Student Composition as Compared to Model Composition

Introduction

The thesis of the student's work contains a good theme statement for the sonnet in the last sentence of paragraph one. The student also indicates the technical elements of form and diction, which will be discussed. However, the ways form and diction are used should be focused and sharpened, as in the italicized portions of the model theme, which carefully indicate each of the ways the techniques will be developed in the succeeding paragraph.

Developmental Paragraph 1

The main problem with this paragraph of the student's theme is that the topic sentence lacks a concept to develop. The first sentence merely describes *what* is in the poem. It does not answer the analytical question of *why* the author wrote the poem that way. The student does, in three places, attempt to answer the question of the author's purpose (see italicized sentences). An overall concept of the sort needed is the rhetorical question-exhortation to conversion idea in the model theme.

Developmental Paragraph 2

The student's topic sentence is adequate although "diction" does not provide a strong focus. This type of topic sentence is acceptable for timed-writing practices but should be refined for an untimed essay. An excellent point is made in the third sentence (italicized section) where the student ties together two word choices in a logical explanation of the author's purpose as it relates to the composition. Four good pieces of evidence appear in the fifth sentence (italicized section) when the student explains how Shakespeare shows us that the body is of no importance. The student begins to develop the metaphor of eating but stops before really getting started, as can be seen by comparing the student's treatment of the discussion of this metaphor in the model composition. The student's final statement about the Death paradox has verve as well as insight.

Conclusion

This is a valid evaluation of the worth of the poem. The student's final statement, though somewhat detached from the rest of the paragraph, is a clever summary.

Lesson 12
Introduction to Stylistic Analysis

Objective

- To have students differentiate two authors' styles by examining their writing techniques

Notes to the Teacher

In the analysis of prose passages, the main question to focus upon is "For what purpose did the author use this stylistic technique?" Identifying a technique is not enough; the technique becomes significant only when it is related to the overall purpose of the passage. Again, students are encouraged to discover which techniques offer the best approach to a particular passage.

Procedure

1. Distribute **Handouts 17** and **18**. Have students, working with partners, read the six selections and apply the worksheet to one pair, one and two, three and four, or five and six.

2. When students have finished, have them share answers with the class so everyone will hear a discussion of all six passages and comparisons among passages can be made.

3. Have students do the writing assignment at the bottom of the handout as a homework assignment.

Suggested Responses:

Passage 1

1. Somewhat outrageous attitude toward money

2. The idea that a virtue of money is that it destroys base people (again, an outrageous attitude)

3. Abstract; all ten nouns

4. No

5. No

6. "Destroys" contrasts with "fortifies and dignifies."

7. "Base" contrasts with "noble." "Conspicuously and undeniably" are vivid.

8. Short length of beginning sentence gives it emphasis.

9. Simple, compound, complex

   Balance is obtained through compound structures and the repeated "as . . . as" constructions.

10. Series of five words used twice in sentence two

11. No symbols

12. No images

13. Pause after announcement of sentence one; other two sentences have inner rhythm

14. Repetition of "represents" and "people" adds to rhythm. Effect is emphasis.

Passage 2

1. Mood is reminiscent, gentle enjoyment.

2. Long series of adjectives before "Christmas"

3. Concrete words like "school-capped," "mufflered," "bright new boots squeaking," and "Jim and Dan and Jack" make experience immediate.

4. "Bedizened" "snowscape" (landscape in snow)

5. First person makes it intimate and personal.

6. Squeaking

7. "Turkey-proud," "school-capped," "mufflered," "silent" (contrasts to talk around fire); lots of adjectives

8. The sentence meanders as the boys do. There is one sentence only, with ninety-six words.

9. Complex sentence with many clause and phrase expanders

10. Adjective series carefully organized—two two-word modifiers; two three-word modifiers; one four-word modifier

11. No symbols

12. Sight—others sat around the fire; white world, silent snowscape of our town Sound—talk/silence, squeaking of boots

13. Yes—Lazy meandering with rich excess of words suggests many luxurious free hours.

14. "Nothing, no nothing"

"when they were children"—conversation

"silent snowscape"—consonance

"crackling"—onomatopoeia

Passage 3

1. Tension, visceral excitement

2. Builds to a climax—pause after "never will," participial phrases build to compound phrase "coming together and crying" and to climactic word "Lord."

3. First half of passage abstract; second half concrete; general statement is followed by specific evidence

4. "Visceral"

5. First person—very personal experience examined for its meaning then and now

6. Participles in last sentence are very forceful.

7. "Exciting" provides attitude. "Blindest" is a vivid word.

8. Sentence one is very short, for emphasis; other two sentences are quite long but easy to comprehend.

9. Sentences are either simple (first and third) or compound (second), which explains the ease of comprehension.

10. Participial phrases in third sentence are a parallel series of four, with last item compounded; effect is to increase excitement.

11. No

12. Sound—"tambourines racing," "sinners moaning," "all those voices coming together and crying holy unto the Lord"

13. Yes—Sentence three is very rhythmical, beginning slowly (almost stopping after "music") and then picking up speed and volume to the end of the passage. This passage recreates the cadence of some preaching.

14. Repetitions—"exciting," "excitement"; "music like that music," "drama like the drama" (pattern repetition as well as word repetition)

Passage 4

1. Impression of a sermon, great solemnity and moral weightiness

2. Passage sounds old-fashioned with its heavy morality and its archaic phrasing.

3. Abstract—two lists of abstractions, all with moral connotations

4. There are many archaic expressions in this passage: "liberty" (instead of freedom), "you would say," "thereon," "was able for," "doing of the same," "be not that," "I for one," and "small care."

5. "I" and "you" are used once, but no intimacy is obtained.

6. No

7. "True liberty," "right path" (moral emphasis)

8. Long; sentence two has twenty-seven words; sentence three has twenty-eight words; sentence four has twenty-four words. Yet balance of sentences makes them easy to comprehend.

9. Sentences two and four are simple, but they contain many phrase expanders, especially infinitives. Sentence three has the same use of infinitive phrases but adds a noun clause to make it complex.

10. Series of three infinitive phrases and series of three abstract nouns in sentence three; series of four abstract nouns in last sentence

11. "Right path" is a cliché symbol.

12. No images

13. Rhythm again moves toward a climax but with interruptions for emphasis.

14. Repetitions include "finding out," "to find out"; "to" of all infinitives; "liberty." Consonance occurs in "permission," "persuasion," "compulsion." Rhythm is also repeated.

Passage 5

1. Impression—pain of wounded on battle field; tone—empathy, anger, regret

2. Enemy and brother are treated alike once they are wounded. The vivid imagery communicates a realization of the pain of the wounded.

3. Concrete—"burden," "blood," "canvas," "stretchers," "arms," "heads"

4. No

5. No

6. Yes—"jounced," "dripping," "shattered," "struggling"

7. Yes—"off step," "hurt," "painfully"

8. Sentence one has forty-one words, yet it is easily comprehended.

9. Sentence one is complex with two dependent clauses and two participial phrases; the pattern of noun, participial phrase, dependent clauses (even repeating "so") is repeated. "Sentence" two is not a complete sentence but two participial phrases with no main verb. Grammar fits sense: the "walking wounded" are also only partially present. Again, the syntax is repeated in this sentence fragment, as is the subject.

10. No

11. No

12. Strong images, already discussed

13. The two halves of sentence one, separated by "and," repeat the same rhythm. Sentence two begins the same rhythmical repetition in the first half, but the second half is deliberately nonrhythmical to fit the sense of the passage.

14. Alliteration and repetition; "walking wounded"

Passage 6

1. Impression—interesting idea explained in a serious but not solemn tone

2. The idea of a cave of the mind is a striking metaphor.

3. Abstract vocabulary makes comprehension somewhat difficult.

4. "Idol" is somewhat archaic.

5. No

6. Yes—"refracts and discolors," "esteems and admires," "preoccupied and predisposed"; verbs used in pairs

7. Pairing continues—"proper and peculiar."

8. The sentence has seventy-four words, but balance prevents the reading from being difficult.

9. After simple sentence one, sentence two is complex with those dependent clauses and a participial phrase that organizes over half of that sentence.

10. Parallel series of four infinitives organizes the last part of the passage.

11. Cave of the mind as a place where the light of nature is distorted symbolizes the distortion of truth by the idiosyncratic working of the individual mind.

12. No

13. Balanced infinitive phrases produce some rhythmical effects.

14. No

Passages for Stylistic Analysis

Passage 1

Money is the most important thing in the world. It represents health, strength, honor, generosity and beauty as conspicuously and undeniably as the want of it represents illness, weakness, disgrace, meanness and ugliness. Not the least of its virtues is that it destroys base people as certainly as it fortifies and dignifies noble people.

From "Preface" to Major Barbara, *George Bernard Shaw*

Passage 2

And I remember that on the afternoon of Christmas Day, when the others sat around the fire and told each other that this was nothing, no nothing, to the great snow-bound and turkey-proud yule-log-crackling holly-berry-bedizened and kissing-under-the-mistletoe Christmas when *they* were children, I would go out, school-capped and gloved and mufflered, with my bright new boots squeaking, into the white world on to the seaward hill, to call on Jim and Dan and Jack and to walk with them through the silent snowscape of our town.

From "Memories of Christmas," Dylan Thomas

Passage 3

The church was very exciting. It took a long time for me to disengage myself from this excitement, and on the blindest, most visceral level, I never really have, and never will. There is no music like that music, no drama like the drama of the saints rejoicing, the sinners moaning, the tambourines racing, and all those voices coming together and crying holy unto the Lord.

From The Fire Next Time, *James Baldwin*

Passage 4

Liberty? The true liberty of a man, you would say, consisted in his finding out, or being forced to find out, the right path, and to walk thereon. To learn, or to be taught, what work he actually was able for; and then by permission, persuasion, and even compulsion, to set about doing of the same! That is his true blessedness, honour, liberty and maximum of wellbeing; if liberty be not that, I for one have small care about liberty.

From "Democracy," Thomas Carlyle

Passage 5

The stretcher-bearers come back from the lines, walking in off step, so that the burden will not be jounced too much, and the blood dripping from the canvas, brother and enemy in the stretchers, so long as they are hurt. And the walking wounded coming back with shattered arms and bandaged heads, the walking wounded struggling painfully to the rear.

From "Battle Scene," John Steinbeck

Passage 6

The Idols of the Cave are the idols of the individual man. For everyone (besides the errors common to human nature in general) has a cave or den of his own, which refracts and discolors the light of nature; owing either to his own proper and peculiar nature or to his education and conversation with others; or to the reading of books, and the authority of those whom he esteems and admires; or to the differences of impressions, accordingly as they take place in a mind preoccupied and predisposed or in a mind indifferent and settled.

From "The Idols of the Mind," Francis Bacon

Prose Analysis

General   1. Describe the impression the whole passage makes upon you: its mood and tone.

2. What is the most striking part of the passage?

Diction   3. Are most of the words abstract or concrete? List some examples.

4. Are there any unfamiliar or unusual words or usages? List them.

5. Does the passage use either first or second person pronouns?

6. Are verbs or verbals especially noticeable? List vivid examples.

7. Are adjectives or adverbs especially vivid? List examples.

Syntax   8. Are the sentences especially long (over twenty words) or short (under eight words)?

9. Are most sentences simple or compound? Are most sentences complex or compound-complex? Are there many prepositional or verbal phrases?

10. Are there parallel series of three, four, or more than four?

Poetic Devices 11. Does the passage use any symbols, i.e., simile or metaphor?

12. Does the passage have any strong images not already discussed? What senses are appealed to by the images?

13. Does rhythm or pace reinforce meaning?

14. Is there alliteration, consonance, assonance, onomatopoeia, or repetition?

For each section, try to discover the author's purpose: why does the author use particular devices? What effect does the author want, and how does it relate to what the author says?

After analyzing your two passages, write two paragraphs comparing and contrasting them. Begin with the passage that you have the most to say about; then discuss the second passage in relation to the first (unlike Shaw, Thomas . . .). Work to identify patterns in the passages and show to what purpose the author uses these patterns.

Or, by copying the syntactical pattern or other significant stylistic elements, imitate the style of the passages. Attempt to use your authors' styles to create effective pieces of writing.

Lesson 13
Reading Essays for Understanding

Objective

- To have students examine the content of two essays

Notes to the Teacher

The two essay excerpts in this lesson are chosen for their disparity in style, attitude, and subject matter. Multiple choice questions both gauge students' understanding and serve as a springboard for discussion.

F. Scott Fitzgerald, dead at the age of forty-four, epitomized the Jazz Age with his meteoric rise to acclaim and his consequent shattering fall from fame, wealth, and reputation. In *The Crack-Up*, published posthumously, Fitzgerald recognizes the sadness in life, hidden beneath its sometimes glittering facade.

Edwin Grant Conklin was first a biological scientist and wrote numerous publications on heredity, environment, evolution, and society. He saw people as social and intellectual beings, and his concern in "Ideals as Goals" was that human beings can succeed only when the ideals of science, art, and religion are incorporated into a single purpose.

Procedure

1. Distribute **Handout 19**. Supply students with background information for this essay (see Notes to the Teacher). Ask students to read and reread the essay until they feel comfortable with its content.

2. Distribute **Handout 20**. Ask students to answer multiple choice questions; then check answers in class. Discuss the support on which the correct responses are based.

Suggested Responses:

1. c	6. c
2. b	7. b
3. a	8. d
4. d	9. b
5. a	10. c

3. Distribute **Handout 21**. Repeat process found in procedure 1.

4. Distribute **Handout 22**. Repeat process found in procedure 2.

Suggested Responses:

1. a	6. c
2. c	7. d
3. c	8. b
4. b	9. c
5. a	10. b

5. Students can generally assess their comprehension of the essays by their number of correct answers.

An Excerpt from F. Scott Fitzgerald's
The Crack-Up

Now a man can crack in many ways—can crack in the head—in which case the power of decisions is taken from you by others! or in the body, when one can but submit to the white hospital world; or in the nerves. William Seabrook in an unsympathetic book tells, with some pride and a moving ending, of how he became a public charge. What led to his alcoholism or was bound up with it, was a collapse of his nervous system. Though the present writer was not so entangled—having at the time not tasted so much as a glass of beer for six months—it was his nervous reflexes that were giving way—too much anger and too many tears.

Moreover, to go back to my thesis that life has a varying offensive, the realization of having cracked was not simultaneous with a blow, but with a reprieve.

Not long before, I had sat in the office of a great doctor and listened to a grave sentence. With what, in retrospect, seems some equanimity, I had gone on about my affairs in the city where I was then living, not caring much, not thinking how much had been left undone, or what would become of this and that responsibility, like people do in books; I was well insured and anyhow I had been only a mediocre caretaker of most of the things left in my hands, even of my talent.

But I had a strong sudden instinct that I must be alone. I didn't want to see any people at all. I had seen so many people all my life—I was an average mixer, but more than average in a tendency to identify myself, my ideas, my destiny, with those of all classes that I came in contact with. I was always saving or being saved—in a single morning I would go through the emotions ascribable to Wellington at Waterloo. I lived in a world of inscrutable hostiles and inalienable friends and supporters.

But now I wanted to be absolutely alone and so arranged a certain insulation from ordinary cares.

It was not an unhappy time. I went away and there were fewer people. I found I was good-and-tired. I could lie around and was glad to, sleeping or dozing sometimes twenty hours a day and in the intervals trying resolutely not to think—instead I made lists—made lists and tore them up, hundreds of lists: of cavalry leaders and football players and cities, and popular tunes and pitchers, and happy times, and hobbies and houses lived in and how many suits since I left the army and how many pairs of shoes (I didn't count the suit I bought in Sorrento that shrunk, nor the pumps and dress shirt and collar that I carried around for years and never wore, because the pumps got damp and grainy and the shirt and collar got yellow and starch-rotted). And lists of women I'd liked, and of the times I had let myself be snubbed by people who had not been my betters in character or ability.

—And then suddenly, surprisingly, I got better.

—And cracked like an old plate as soon as I heard the news.

That is the real end of this story. What was to be done about it will have to rest in what used to be called the "womb of time." Suffice it to say that after about an hour of solitary pillow-hugging, I began to realize that for two years my life had been a drawing on resources that I did not possess, that I had been mortgaging myself physically and spiritually up to the hilt. What was the small gift of life given back in comparison to that!—where there had once been a pride of direction and a confidence in enduring independence.

Understanding Fitzgerald's Essay

Circle the correct answer.

1. Fitzgerald sees as the cause for his break-down
   a. alcoholism
   b. loneliness
   c. excessive emotion
   d. the inability to make decisions

2. By using the phrase "life has a varying offensive," Fitzgerald means
   a. life has its ups and downs
   b. life has different levels of pain and struggle
   c. life is hopeless
   d. life has different meanings to each person

3. When Fitzgerald is told of his mental illness, he
   a. accepts the diagnosis calmly
   b. worries about unfinished goals
   c. wonders how long he will live
   d. tries to get his affairs in order

4. His decision to be alone
   a. is not a healthy reaction
   b. results from his always being in a crowd
   c. results from his army experience
   d. is an immediate realization of a natural need

5. Fitzgerald's ability to sleep twenty hours a day
   a. provides a form of escape from thinking
   b. increased his energy
   c. was needed rest from work
   d. provided him time to think

6. In Fitzgerald's description of the lists he made, we learn that
   a. he focused mainly on reasons for his illness
   b. he was practicing good therapy
   c. he was in a sense cataloging his life
   d. he had a variety of interests

7. With his imagery of "cracked like an old plate," Fitzgerald
   a. indicates total destruction
   b. summarizes the natural result of overuse
   c. considers himself as a common object
   d. asks sympathy of his age

8. Fitzgerald's "hour of solitary pillow-hugging"
   a. is an indication of self-pity
   b. illustrates his childishness
   c. shows his desperation
   d. provides his catharsis

9. At the end of this excerpt, Fitzgerald
   a. is grateful for another chance at life
   b. senses his quality of life is forever altered
   c. realizes he has been spending too much money
   d. is now dependent upon others

10. In this essay, Fitzgerald reviews a painful experience of
    a. an airplane accident
    b. personal tragedy
    c. introspection
    d. facing reality

An Excerpt from Edwin Grant Conklin's "Ideals as Goals"

If civilization is to advance, education from the earliest years must develop ideals of love rather than hate, human brotherhood rather than class, racial or national conflicts, peace rather than war, service rather than selfishness. It must instill reverence not only for truth but also for beauty and righteousness. Doubters and cynics will say that these ideals are pleasant dreams, impossible of realization, but the well-known fact that they have been made real in many persons, families, and communions shows that they are possible of fulfillment and that it is only necessary to extend this process of education to wider and larger groups to bring a new and better spirit into the world.

Human progress consists not only in right thinking, but also in right feeling and doing. A proper combination of all these is necessary for the most useful and happy living. Science properly seeks to eliminate emotions while engaged in the search for truth. For this very reason the scientist more than many others needs to cultivate the emotions that find their highest expression in art, music, poetry, religion. Charles Darwin, in that part of his *Autobiography* which was written in the last year of his life, confessed that formerly he took great delight in poetry, pictures and music, but that now for many years he could not bear to read a line of poetry, and that he had lost his taste for pictures and music. He says:

> . . . *My mind seems to have become a kind of machine for grinding out general laws . . . If I had to live my life again I would make it a rule to read some poetry and to listen to some music at least once every week. The loss of these tastes is a loss of happiness, and may possibly be injurious to the intellect, and more probably to the moral character, by enfeebling the moral part of our nature.*

Other scientists have had a similar experience, but some, unlike Darwin, do not regret it and seem to be proud of the fact that they are superior to such aesthetic emotions. One can only pity them for a loss which they do not realize.

The greatest problems that confront mankind are how to promote social cooperation, how to increase loyalty to truth, how to promote justice, how to expand ethics until it embraces all mankind. These are problems for science as well as for government, education, and religion. Each of these agencies has its own proper function to perform. Science as well as religion includes both faith and works, ideals and their realization. The faith, ideals and ethics of science constitute a form of natural religion.[1]

---

[1]Edwin Grant Conklin, "Ideals as Goals," *Man, Real and Ideal* (New York: Charles Scribner's Sons, 1943).

Name_____

Date _____

Understanding Conklin's Essay

Circle the correct answer.

1. Conklin believes that education
   a. is responsible for the advancement of civilization
   b. should teach moral responsibility
   c. is unrealistic in its goals
   d. is the inalienable right of all people

2. In this essay excerpt, Conklin begins with
   a. comparisons
   b. contradictions
   c. contrasts
   d. complexities

3. According to Conklin,
   a. most people will reject his ideas
   b. his proposal is idealistic
   c. his proposal is entirely possible
   d. only an intellectual can understand his ideas

4. Conklin believes the scientist is right to
   a. follow Darwin's theory of evolution
   b. omit emotion while searching for truths
   c. become emotionally involved in work
   d. proceed without emotion in daily life

5. Conklin notes that Charles Darwin
   a. wished he had regularly read poetry and listened to music
   b. read poetry and listened to music daily
   c. regrets he read poetry or listened to music
   d. wrote both poetry and music

6. The reference to Darwin reveals that he
   a. bettered himself through poetry and music
   b. felt poetry and music were harmful to science
   c. felt poetry and music enriched happiness
   d. was weakened morally by poetry and music

7. Conklin says some other scientists are
   a. proud of their scientific discoveries
   b. disdainful of Darwin's evolution theory
   c. sorry they were not poets or musicians
   d. proud they have no sensitivity to the arts

8. Speaking of mankind's problems, Conklin
   a. dismisses them as unscientific
   b. says the problems are a concern of science
   c. admits science has its own set of problems
   d. suggests that science can solve most problems

9. Conklin says that science
   a. has no responsibility to religion
   b. shares responsibility with education
   c. includes faith, work, and realization of ideals
   d. should be a separate governmental agency

10. In this essay, Conklin explores the idea that
    a. emotions are detrimental to scientific pursuit
    b. humanity's welfare must be a common goal for all
    c. religion and science are incompatible
    d. humanity's welfare is science's proper function

Lesson 14
Written Analysis of Essays

Objective

• To give students an opportunity to affirm their knowledge of essays through written analysis

Notes to the Teacher

Many educators believe that learning is not complete until what has been studied can be written about effectively. Adhering to that belief, this lesson asks students to write analytical compositions on the essays of Fitzgerald and Conklin. Refer to Lesson 5, which illustrates the structure suggested for organization of the writing process.

Procedure

1. Encourage students that by now they have a thorough knowledge of the content of the essays by Fitzgerald and Conklin, and they are ready to write compositions analyzing these essays.

2. Assign analytical compositions centered on the following questions about the essays of Fitzgerald and/or Conklin. Remind students the compositions should be unified with an introduction, thesis statement, central idea, and topic sentences, all progressing to a logical conclusion. Refer also to those points in **Handout 18** that are applicable to this assignment. These compositions can be completed either during class or as homework.

a. What does each writer reveal about himself or human nature in general?

b. What is the author's attitude toward his subject? Toward the reader?

c. Is the essayist sharing a confidence or a theory?

d. What is the purpose of each of the essays?

e. What is the effect of the personal or impersonal style each uses?

f. What is the difference in vocabulary in the essays? How effective is the choice of diction and syntax?

g. Which author is more convincing in his approach?

h. Which essay is more readable? Why?

Lesson 15
Timed Writings on Prose Passages

Objective

- To provide students with practice in timed writings responding to nonfictional passages

Notes to the Teacher

The ability to complete well-written, impromptu, timed essays is the key to successful completion of the Advanced Placement examination. Practicing timed writings develops several skills to students: rapid assessment of the meaning, logic, and style of a selection; relating a specific question to the selection; producing a well-written and perceptive essay response. The impromptu essay challenges the students' ability to "think on their feet"!

This lesson is accompanied by four handouts, each of which requires a complete class period. You may want to select among them or use all of them either consecutively or occasionally.

Procedure

1. Tell students that this lesson will provide practice in the skill of impromptu composition. Point out that they will receive copies of an essay question and that they will have thirty-five minutes to complete the essay.

2. Distribute **Handout 23**, **24**, **25**, or **26**, and direct students to begin working. Make a note of the starting time.

3. Exactly thirty-five minutes later, tell students to stop working, and collect the essays.

4. Essay evaluation may take place in several ways. Traditional grading helps provide an objective and authoritative viewpoint. Self-grading minimizes threat and enables students to discover and correct their own weaknesses. Peer-grading stimulates development of new perspective and enables students to benefit from the critical advice of a variety of readers. **Handout 27** may be helpful to both you and your students in completing evaluations.

Timed Writing Practice

The following commentary by newscaster Eric Sevareid, written in 1958, reflects the modern era's concern with the relationship between technological advance and human development. Read the selection carefully. Then write an essay in which you deal with the same topic from the point of view of the 1990s, and show how your viewpoint agrees with or contradicts Sevareid's. Include specific references to his ideas, diction, and use of detail.

The Dark of the Moon
Eric Sevareid

This, thank goodness, is the first warm and balmy night of the year in these parts; the first frogs are singing. Altogether this is hardly the night for whispering sweet sentiments about the reciprocal trade act, the extension thereof. But since we are confined, by tradition, to the contemplation of public themes and issues, let us contemplate the moon. The lovely and luminous moon has become a public issue. For quite a few thousand years it was a private issue; it figured in purely bilateral negotiations between lovers, in the incantations of jungle witch doctors and Indian corn planters. Poets from attic windows issued the statements about the moon, and they made better reading than the Mimeographed handouts now being issued by assistant secretaries of defense.

The moon was always measured in terms of hope and reassurance and the heart pangs of youth on such a night as this; it is now measured in terms of mileage and foot-pounds of rocket thrust. Children sent sharp, sweet wishes to the moon; now they dream of blunt-nosed missiles.

There must come a time, in every generation, when those who are older secretly get off the train of progress, willing to walk back to where they came from, if they can find the way. We're afraid we're getting off now. Cheer, if you wish, the first general or Ph.D. who splatters something on the kindly face of the moon. We shall grieve for him, for ourself, for the young lovers and poets and dreams to come, because the ancient moon will never be the same again. There, we suspect, the heart of man will never be the same.

We find it very easy to wait for the first photographs of the other side of the moon, for we have not yet seen the other side of Lake Louise or the Blue Ridge peak that shows through the cabin window.

We find ourself quite undisturbed about the front-page talk of "controlling the earth from the moon," because we do not believe it. If neither men nor gadgets nor both combined can control the earth from the earth, we fail to see how they will do so from the moon.

It is exciting talk, indeed, the talk of man's advance toward space. But one little step in man's advance toward man—that, we think, would be truly exciting. Let those who wish try to discover the composition of a lunar crater; we would settle for discovering the true mind of a Russian commissar or the inner heart of a delinquent child.

There is, after all, another side—a dark side—to the human spirit, too. Men have hardly begun to explore these regions; and it is going to be a very great pity if we advance upon the bright side of the moon with the dark side of ourselves, if the cargo in the first rockets to reach there consists of fear and chauvinism and suspicion. Surely we ought to have our credentials in order, our hands very clean and perhaps a prayer for forgiveness on our lips as we prepare to open the ancient vault of the shining moon. [1]

1958

[1]Eric Sevareid, "The Dark of the Moon," *America: 20th Century Exposition Man and the Social Machine* (New York: Don Congdon Associates, Inc., 1973).

Name_____

Date _____

Timed Writing Practice

The following passage is taken from a letter Mark Twain wrote replying to a request to use his name in advertising a play based on Tom Sawyer. Read the selection carefully. Then write an essay in which you describe Twain's attitude toward himself, Tom Sawyer, and No. 1365. Show how Twain's use of language helps to communicate his attitude.

Now as I understand it, dear and magnanimous 1365, you are going to re-create Tom Sawyer dramatically, and then do me the compliment to put me in the bills as father of this shady offspring. Sir, do you know that this kind of compliment has destroyed people before now? Listen.

Twenty-four years ago, I was strangely handsome. The remains of it are still visible through the rifts of time. I was so handsome that human activities ceased as if spellbound when I came in view, and even inanimate things stopped to look—like locomotives, and district messenger boys and so on. In San Francisco, in rainy season I was often mistaken for fair weather. Upon one occasion I was traveling in the Sonora region, and stopped for an hour's nooning, to rest my horse and myself. All the town came out to look. A Piute squaw named her baby for me,—a voluntary compliment which pleased me greatly.

Other attentions were paid me. Last of all arrived the president and faculty of Sonora University and offered me the post of Professor of Moral Culture and Dogmatic Humanities; which I accepted gratefully, and entered at once upon my duties. But my name had pleased the Indians, and in the deadly kindness of their hearts they went on naming their babies after me. I tried to stop it, but the Indians could not understand why I should object to so manifest a compliment. The thing grew and grew and spread and spread and became exceedingly embarrassing. The University stood it a couple of years; but then for the sake of the college they felt obliged to call a halt, although I had the sympathy of the whole faculty.

The president himself said to me, "I am as sorry as I can be for you, and would still hold out if there were any hope ahead; but you see how it is; there are a hundred and thirty-two of them already, and fourteen precincts to hear from. The circumstance has brought your name into most wide and unfortunate renown. It causes much comment—I believe that that is not an overstatement. Some of this comment is palliative, but some of it—by patrons at a distance, who only know the statistics without the explanation—is offensive, and in some cases even violent. Nine students have been called home. The trustees of the college have been growing more and more uneasy all these last months—steadily along with the implacable increase in your census—and I will not conceal from you that more than once they have touched upon the expediency of a change in the Professorship of Moral Culture. The coarsely sarcastic editorial in yesterday's Alta,—headed Give the Moral Acrobat a Rest—has brought things to a crisis, and I am charged with the unpleasant duty of receiving your resignation."

I know you only mean me a kindness, dear 1365, but it is a most deadly mistake. Please do not name your Injun for me.

Timed Writing Practice

Read the following passage carefully. In a well-organized essay, analyze the author's use and explanation of a paradox. Expand the author's explanation with examples and clarifications of your own.

Section III

Another contrast is equally essential for the understanding of ideals—the contrast between order as the condition for excellence, and order as stifling the freshness of living. This contrast is met with in the theory of education. The condition for excellence is a thorough training in technique. Sheer skill must pass out of the sphere of conscious exercise, and must have assumed the character of unconscious habit. The first, the second, and the third condition for high achievement is scholarship, in that enlarged sense including knowledge and acquired instinct controlling action.

The paradox which wrecks so many promising theories of education is that the training which produces skill is so very apt to stifle imaginative zest. Skill demands repetition, and imaginative zest is tinged with impulse. Up to a certain point each gain in skill opens new paths for the imagination. But in each individual, formal training has its limit of usefulness. Beyond that limit there is degeneration: 'The lilies of the field toil not, neither do they spin.'

The social history of mankind exhibits great organizations in their alternating functions of conditions for progress, and of contrivances for stunting humanity. The history of the Mediterranean lands, and of western Europe, is the history of the blessing and the curse, of political organizations, of religious organizations, of schemes of thought, of social agencies for large purposes. The moment of dominance, prayed for, worked for, sacrificed for, by generations of the noblest spirits, marks the turning point where the blessing passes into the curse. Some new principle of refreshment is required. The art of progress is to preserve order amid change, and to preserve change amid order. Life refuses to be embalmed alive. The more prolonged the halt in some unrelieved system of order, the greater the crash of the dead society.[2]

[2]Alfred North Whitehead, *Process and Reality* (New York: Macmillan Publishing Co., Inc., 1978), 338–339.

Timed Writing Practice

In an 1833 letter to John Stuart Mill, Victorian writer Thomas Carlyle included the following description of thirty-year-old Ralph Waldo Emerson.

> Emerson, Your Presentee, rolled up hither, one still Sunday afternoon while we sat at dinner. A most gentle, recommendable, amiable, whole-hearted man; whom we thank for one of the pleasantest interruptions to our solitude. He staid with us four-and-twenty hours; and was thro' the whole Encyclopedia with us in that time. A good "Socinian" understanding, the clearest heart; above all, what I loved in the man was his health, his unity with himself; all people and all things seemed to find their quite peaceable adjustment with him, not a proud domineering one, as after doubtful *contest*, but a spontaneous-looking, peaceable, even humble one I should henceforth learn to see, or see better, that Unitarians are not hollow men, but at worst limited men, and otherwise of the fairest conditions. Their very need of a religion, strongly evinced by that creed of theirs, should recommend them. One seems to believe almost all that they believe; and when they stop short and call it Religion, and you pass on, and call it only a reminiscence of one should you not part with the kiss of peace?

Fourteen years later, following another visit by Emerson, Carlyle wrote a letter to a Mrs. Baring, including this excerpt about Emerson.

> I was torn to pieces, talking with him; for his sad Yankee rule seemed to be, that talk should go on incessantly except when sleep interrupted it; a frightful rule. The man, as you have heard is not above a bargain; nor, if one will be candid, is he fairly much below it. A pure-minded elevated man; elevated but without breadth, as a willow is, as a reed is; no fruit at all to be gathered from him. A delicate, but thin pinched triangular face, no jaws nor lips, lean-hooked nose; face of a *cock*: by none such was the Thames ever burnt! A proud man too; a certain sensitive fastidious *stickishness*, which reminded me of a miniature Washington's, very exotic tho' Anglo-Saxon enough; rather curious to think of. No getting into any intimacy with him, talk as you will. You have my leave to fall in love with him if you can! And so he plays his part: gone to lecture in Lancashire; to return hither he knows not when: it is privately hoped he may go to Rome! I wish him honestly well, do as I am bound respect him honestly; but *Friends*, it is clear, we can never in this world, to any real purpose, be.

In a well-organized essay, compare and contrast the two views of Emerson. Consider point of view, audience, and use of language in both passages.

Name_____

Date _____

Evaluation Checklist

Response to Eric Sevareid

	Excellent	Good	Adequate	Weak	Poor
1. Direct recognition of Sevareid's emphasis on human development, lest technological advancement become destructive					
2. Direct statement of student's view of relationship between technological development and human development					
3. Citation of specific points of agreement/ disagreement					
4. Logical development of personal view					
5. Correct grammar and usage					
6. Effective word choice, phrasing, and personal style					
7. Unity and coherence					

Evaluation Checklist

Dealing with Mark Twain

	Excellent	Good	Adequate	Weak	Poor
1. Direct recognition of Twain's use of satire					
2. Recognition of Twain's self-confidence and wit					
3. Recognition of Twain's humorous mocking at No. 1365					
4. Correct grammar and usage					
5. Effective word choice, phrasing, and personal style					
6. Unity and coherence					
7. Use of specific language references					

Evaluation Checklist

The Paradox of Order

	Excellent	Good	Adequate	Weak	Poor
1. Identification of the paradox that order both cultivates excellence and oppresses it					
2. Recognition of application to education					
3. Recognition of application to history and change					
4. Recognition of synthesis of order and change					
5. Inclusion of original examples and clarifications					
6. Use of thesis and topic sentences					
7. Correct grammar and usage					
8. Effective word choice, phrasing, and personal style					
9. Unity and coherence					

Name_____

Date _____

Evaluation Checklist

Carlyle and Emerson

	Excellent	Good	Adequate	Weak	Poor
1. Identification of specific similarities in descriptions					
2. Identification of specific differences					
3. Recognition of changes in Carlyle himself					
4. Recognition of possible effects of different audiences					
5. Inclusion of specific language references					
6. Clear thesis statement					
7. Logical development					
8. Correct grammar and usage					
9. Effective word choice, phrasing, and personal style					
10. Unity and coherence					

Lesson 16
Greek Tragedy and the World from Which It Came

Objective

- To aid students in relating Greek tragedies to the culture that produced them

Notes to the Teacher

This lesson assumes a thorough reading and class discussion of the Greek tragedy, *Oedipus the King* by Sophocles. After students understand the play, they are ready to see it as embodying the ideas current at the time it was written.

Procedure

1. Lead a discussion about ways the Greek stage affected the writing and performance of Greek tragedies. The following are some ideas to consider.

   a. In general, since plays were given in a very large open-air amphitheater, detail in characterization, movement, or plot development was impossible. All delineation had to be large and broad to simplify and clarify what happened on stage. Specifically mention the use of masks, the limited number of actors used (focused action), and stage movement confined to broad actions.

   b. The fact that there was no curtain resulted in minimal scenery. The procession of the chorus on and off stage while singing parados, exodos, and choral odes was used to separate scenes.

   c. At center stage was an altar to Dionysus, ensuring that some reference to the gods be made. (Originally, drama was ritual worship of the gods, but practice took drama away from worship and toward the questioning of social and religious order.)

2. Distribute **Handout 28,** and allow students time to read it.

3. Write on the board this statement from Edith Hamilton's *The Greek Way:*

   > *"Sophocles is the embodiment of all we know as Greek, so much so that all definitions of the Greek spirit and Greek art are first of all definitions of his spirit and his art."*

   Explain that Aristotle based his analysis of tragedy in his *Poetics* upon Sophocles's *Oedipus.* Focus on Aristotle's definition of "unity of action," which dictates that a plot be constructed so that no scene can be eliminated without breaking the chain of cause and effect. Ask students to show how the action of each scene in *Oedipus* is essential to the logic of the plot.

Suggested Responses:

Prologue	*Oedipus and Creon*	*Problem stated: Oedipus curses murderer.*
Scene 1	*Oedipus and Tiresias*	*Tiresias accuses Oedipus, but Oedipus refuses to believe him.*
Scene 2	*Oedipus, Creon, Jocasta*	*Oedipus hears that Laius's murder occurred where three roads meet.*
Scene 3	*Corinthian Messenger, Oedipus*	*Oedipus hears the "good news" of Polybus's death; he then discovers that he himself was abandoned and adopted as an infant.*
Scene 4	*Shepherd, Corinthian Messenger, Oedipus*	*Oedipus discovers that he was Laius's son, since he was the baby given to the shepherd by Jocasta.*
Scene 5	*Messenger, Oedipus, Creon*	*Jocasta commits suicide; Oedipus blinds himself.*

4. Tell students they have reviewed, through their plot analysis, the ideas current in Greek culture at the time *Oedipus* was written.

5. Instruct students to make a list of all the ways *Oedipus* embodies the ideas current in Greek culture at the time it was written.

Suggested Responses:

a. *Know thyself*—Oedipus is the classic example of the human whose central problem is not knowing himself/herself.

   "Nothing in excess" and *hubris*—Oedipus is so proud of his mental powers that he challenges the gods.

   "Man is the measure"—Oedipus tries to defy the oracles, as does Jocasta, but they are proven wrong.

b. *Polarities*—Oedipus experiences fame and shame, sight and blindness, and ignorance and insight.

   Wholeness—The play exemplifies unity of dramatic action.

   Mind—Oedipus's great strength as well as his downfall is his search for truth.

c. *Freedom*—Oedipus's first address to his people shows him to be concerned for their health and welfare.

   Oedipus has freedom to try to beat the prophecy of the gods.

   Tiresias has no power over him.

d. *Retributive justice*—Justice is restored when Oedipus is punished for killing his father and for questioning the gods.

   Religion is directed toward the needs of the state rather than the individual—Oedipus's exposure as the murderer of Laius satisfies Apollo's desire for justice so the plague can cease.

e. *Fate controls the lives of humanity*—This is obvious in the case of Oedipus. In modern terms, the "unjust" gods may stand for circumstantial and destructive forces over which we have no control.

6. Have each student read another Greek play and write a composition showing how the play embodies Greek thought as it has been discussed in class.

   Suggestions:

Aeschylus	*Oresteia Trilogy*
	Electra
Sophocles	*Antigone*
	Oedipus at Colonus
	Electra
Euripides	*Medea*
	The Trojan Women
	Hippolytus
	Electra

The Miracle That Was Greece

For about one hundred years, from 480 to 380 B.C., a remarkable culture existed in the city-state of Athens. There individuals realized the power of their minds to examine their environment and themselves. It is difficult for us, reason-oriented people of the twentieth century, to realize the difference between the fear of all things unknown that existed before this time and the confidence that everything can be known, which is our attitude, as well as that of the classical Greeks, who were the first moderns.

Such an explosion of creative and intellectual genius as occurred during the Golden Age of Greece cannot happen unless the circumstances are exactly right. The following historical events helped prepare for the miraculous one hundred years, when classical Greece was at its height:

1. Many local town councils in Attica were reorganized into a united council to center government administration in Athens.

2. A harsh code of law published in 621 B.C. by Draco was criticized by Solon, with the result that Solon himself was given the powers of a dictator to make economic and political reforms.

3. All male citizens were voting members of the only legislative body, the Assembly, whose administrators were chosen by drawing lots.

4. National festivals, such as the Festival of Dionysus for drama, gave the citizens a shared communal ritualistic experience.

5. The Athenean fleet provided protection for the League of Aegean city-states headquartered in Athens in exchange for payment by members; this money built magnificent public buildings, such as the Parthenon and others on the Acropolis, under the direction of Pericles, whose goal was to make Athens the cultural as well as the intellectual and political center of Greece.

6. Atheneans prized leisure more than material goods; the resulting asceticism, combined with a slave economy, led to much leisure time to cultivate social and intellectual life.[1]

Within this environment grew a new exuberant breed of people, who were in love with life and filled with creative energy. From these people in this culture came some rich new ideas about how humanity relates to its own self, to the environment, and to the gods.

First, the Athenians acknowledged the mystery that is within and around humans. "Know thyself," was one of two sentences inscribed at the temple in Delphi. The second, and a corollary to this introspection, was "Nothing in excess," advice to strive for moderation as the way to exist in the proper role of humankind, between the extremes of animal and god. The Greeks knew they would be tempted to be less than their rational selves. The extremes of drunken orgy or madness depicted in some of the tragedies

[1]H.D.F. Kitto, *The Greeks* (Chicago: Aldine Publishing Co., 1964), passim 98–108.

show how people can cross the line separating humanity from beasts. On the other hand, heroes of Greek tragedy sometimes cross the line separating humanity from divinity and arrogantly assume they are more than human, an excess of hubris or pride as they challenge the gods themselves. Yet a proper perspective on their own nature gave the Greeks a healthy confidence in their own powers. "Man is the measure of all things," they confidently believed. This signaled a new philosophy for a mind-centered human in a human-centered universe. Unknown gods did not measure and punish humanity, but humanity provided the only criterion for itself. Such a criterion was *arete*, best translated as excellence in whatever form was most appropriate (i.e., personal courage for the warrior). But *arete* is more than excellence; it implies the very highest that a human being can attain, with the added assumption that such perfection naturally has a compelling quality once it is perceived.

Second, the Greek's self-confidence came from the discovery of the miracle of the mind. Rationality now replaced former ignorance, magic, and fear. The Greek observed everything in sight and then thought about it. This is the method of science, which had its beginnings in Athenean Greece. The Western habit of mind, born in Greece, sees reality in terms of polarities or opposites, in contrast to the Eastern mind, which approaches reality as one undifferentiated whole. Through the western type of polarization of ideas, refinement of thought often occurs.

At the same time, the quality of the Greek mind compelled it to find connections, order, and synthesis rather than to focus on particulars. Matthew Arnold described the Greek approach as the capacity to "see things clearly and to see them whole." Perhaps this tendency is best recognized through architecture: Greeks placed their temples on hilltops so that the building and its surroundings would be a unity. The temple itself is clean-lined with simple columns, a carved pediment, and an unbroken, symmetrical roofline clearly visible from miles away. Detail and decoration are not the focus, as they are in a Gothic cathedral; the Greeks' goal was the perfectly formed whole building and environment.

In drama, the same tendency to see things whole is reflected in the adherence to the three unities. The three great writers of Greek tragedies, Aeschylus, Sophocles, and Euripedes, unconsciously followed these rules, which were later formulated by Aristotle. First, unity of place dictates that a play has only one setting; unity of time dictates that there is no break in the time of the action; unity of action dictates that the plot is so tightly constructed that no scene can be removed without damaging the logic of cause and effect. All three of the unities work toward an overall clarity and simplicity of effect so that the dramatic impact will be greater.

Third, the love of life was expressed through an emphasis upon the fitness of the physical body and play, as exemplified in the Olympic games. Beauty for the Greeks consisted in the physical (what is seen) not the symbolic (what is not seen). Greek art stressed physical beauty; the gods are sculpted as perfectly formed men and women of great beauty.

Fourth, the Atheneans arranged their social institutions to provide them with a maximum degree of freedom, established in two ways:

1. freedom from the domination of a political power; the pure Athenian democracy placed government in the hands of amateurs but guaranteed absolute freedom from political oppression;

2. freedom from domination of priests and fear of the supernatural; the Greeks were free to use their minds as far as they would go in the area of religion.

Fifth, the temper of the Greek mind rejected any orthodoxy in religion so that the polytheism of the Olympic gods prevailed for many years. However, the best thinkers among the philosophers and poets went beyond it to monotheism or, in the case of Euripedes, toward rebellion. The Athenean mind enjoyed Homer's Olympians, the antics of Zeus and his amours, and the trickery of the gods during the Trojan War when they fought for their favorite heroes. Going beyond the Homeric concept of the justice (or whimsy) of Zeus, Aeschylus developed the idea of retributive justice (*dike*) in which balance and order reassert themselves in the universe because of the influence of Zeus. However, mortals had little hope of influencing the gods; mortals could not communicate personal needs to the gods but only submit to them. The gods did communicate with mortals through Apollo's oracle in one of two ways: either through a prophecy coming from a priestess who was possessed by the spirit of god and who spoke for him, or through prophets who could read signs and interpret the god's message to humanity. In general, religion was oriented toward the needs of the city-state, not the individual soul, except in the case of the Orphic cults or the Eleusinian mysteries.

Sixth, the Greek idea of fate acknowledged the many happenings in human lives that are beyond human power to control or explain in terms of "just dessert," i.e., the natural disasters that kill innocent people. The Greeks personified fate as Moirai, which overruled even Zeus, and as three women: Atropos, who cuts the thread of life at death; Clotho, who spins the thread of life for the living; and Lachesis, who casts lots to place a child at birth.

The Greek understanding of the mixture of fate and freedom in every human's life may be illustrated by the situation of a dog chained to a post. The dog's freedom is limited by the chain, which allows it to circle the post. Within the circle, the dog has freedom of movement but cannot go outside it. Similarly, the circumstances of an individual's life determine the radius of his or her circle of limitations.

Athenian loss to Sparta in the Peloponnesian Wars led to a great moral breakdown in Athens, and the brief flare of glory was over. Such genius in a nation was not to be seen again until the rediscovery of the Greek miracle in the Renaissance.

Lesson 17

The Elizabethan Renaissance and William Shakespeare

Objective

- To enable students to recognize characteristics of the Renaissance through study of two Shakespearean plays

Notes to the Teacher

The England of William Shakespeare's time was the result of several generations of general upheaval. By the year of Shakespeare's birth in 1564, England had undergone major revisions in religion as a result of the Reformation. By 1564, the social structure known as feudalism had gradually been shattered, so there was greater mobility for the masses of common people. Copernicus had determined a new center of the universe, and the human mind had reached out to new frontiers of thought.

By 1564, the Renaissance, begun in Italy and spreading northward throughout Europe during the 1400s, had reached England's shores with tremendous impact. Change was the by-word, as increased intellectual activity produced new discoveries, explorations, and inventions. In London, William Caxton's printing press was ready to spread these findings far afield.

William Shakespeare was born into a climate rich in humanistic ideals. His birthplace, Stratford-on-Avon, was no longer an isolated village. Troupes of players performed theatrical productions there, providing the young Shakespeare with a glimpse of the world of imagination that awaited him.

There is no absolute authority on the reasons why Shakespeare left his wife and children in Stratford, but records indicate that by the age of 28, in 1592, he was a recognized writer and part-time actor in London theater. He had had little preparation for his craft, which reinforces the belief in his natural genius and his embodiment of the humanistic ideal.

Shakespeare was in a unique position of being the right individual in the right place at the right time. Three factors greatly aided in preparing the soil in which he would germinate. First, after the date of her coronation in 1558, Elizabeth I achieved peace and unity in England, thus creating more time for intellectual pursuits, which the Queen heartily endorsed. Secondly, the church, in its morality and miracle plays, had for years dramatized scriptural lessons, which, when coupled with the advent of the interest in literature, provided fertile ground for the development of drama. Thirdly, the construction of the first theater, aptly named The Theater, in 1576, provided recognition of drama as a permanent art form and endowed its participants with a certain degree of respectability.

Into this scene strode the gifted and talented William Shakespeare. The world has reeled from the impact for more than 350 years, supporting Ben Jonson's observation that "He was not of an age, but for all time."

Procedure

1. Review what students already know about Shakespeare's life, his development as a playwright, the wide variety of his thirty-seven plays, the Shakespearean audience, the Shakespearean theater, and other details concerning Shakespeare himself and his contribution to literature. This information is readily available in any collections of his works, school texts, filmstrips, encyclopedias, etc.

2. Make sure students understand that comedy, in the Shakespearean sense, refers to that drama wherein the main character is successful. Tragedy refers to that drama wherein the main character is doomed to failure through his or her own flaw.

3. Using your own judgment, make sure students are familiar with the play, *The*

Tempest. You may do this in a variety of ways, but keep in mind that Shakespeare's plays are meant to be heard, not just read silently. Reading the play can be supplemented with audiovisual aids. Further steps in the procedure assume that students have a solid understanding of the play.

4. Have students read and discuss the information contained on **Handout 29**. Ask students to add to the examples or create new categories of their own. Ask students to locate within the play the examples used on the handout. If you prefer, you may write the categories on the board and have students find examples from the play on their own.

5. Have students write well-organized essays based on one or more of the following topics either for homework or during class.
   a. Indicate how Shakespeare envisioned a better world. Use lines from *The Tempest* as support.
   b. Consider the emphasis Shakespeare places on the intellect and study within *The Tempest*. Discuss his reasons for this emphasis.
   c. Select one area from **Handout 29,** and discuss its importance in the play as a whole.
   d. Trace the behavioral changes of one major character through the course of *The Tempest*. Discuss the effect of these changes.
   e. Use the literary definition of comedy to illustrate a plausible theme of this play.

6. Repeat procedure 3 with *Othello*.

7. Use **Handout 30,** and repeat procedure 4 with *Othello*.

8. Have students write well-organized essays based on one or more of the following topics either for homework or during class.
   a. Discuss the consequences of revenge or jealousy in *Othello*.
   b. Formulate an opinion on cultural or racial biases found in *Othello*. Support your opinion with specific lines from the play.
   c. Answer these questions about the tragedy of the play: Why is Othello doomed to failure? What is his character flaw? Could he have averted disaster?
   d. Trace the use of Desdemona's handkerchief as an item of continuity within the play.
   e. Describe Iago's personality and his motives as the play progresses.

Papers may be written individually or in pairs.

Optional Activities

1. Research costuming requirements of either play. Present your findings to the class.

2. Research music or musical instruments popular during the age of the Renaissance. Share your knowledge through a presentation which includes audio and visual aids.

3. Make a study of athletic events popular during the Renaissance. Share your information with classmates.

4. Write a list of questions to be asked of any of the characters of either play or Shakespeare. Find a partner and conduct the interview.

5. Predict the future for Ferdinand and Miranda. Share your predictions.

6. Describe the perfect modern society in an essay to be shared with classmates.

Elements of the Elizabethan Renaissance Found in
The Tempest

Geographical Expansion/Travel → Setting located on fictional, unexplored island, placed somewhere between Africa and Italy

Superiority of Intellect → Prospero, the learned man, rules over Caliban, the savage, on whom education has been wasted

Interest in Scholarship → Prospero neglects governing Milan, preferring his studies; Prospero leaves Milan with his treasured library

Classical Interest in Greek and Roman Culture → Roman goddesses Juno, Ceres, and Iris appear at Prospero's command

Interest in Human Behavior → The romance of Ferdinand and Miranda; the comic antics of Trinculo and Stephano; Prospero's forgiveness of the King and his followers

Interest in Science/Magic → Prospero promises to bury his staff, rejecting magic

Other elements to look for

Interest in Theology

Human Frailties Revealed in Nobility

Military Technology

Concept of Honor

Name_____

Date _____

Elements of the Elizabethan Renaissance Found in
Othello

Geographical Expansion/Travel → Othello travels from northern Africa to Italy; Othello recounts strange sights he has seen in foreign lands

Interest in Scholarship → Cassio has studied warfare from books but has not actively participated

Classical Interest in Greek and Roman Culture → References to Janus, Prometheus, the Hydra, and Caesar

Interest in Human Behavior → Desdemona as a victim of Othello's jealousy; Iago's manipulation of other characters; Emilia's loyalty to Desdemona

Interest in Science/Magic → Brabantio accuses Othello of using magic to win Desdemona; Iago refers to the poppy plant and its tranquilizing properties

Other elements to look for

Interest in Theology

Concept of Honor

Human Frailties Revealed in Nobility

Superiority of Intellect

Military Technology

Lesson 18
Modern Drama

Objective

- To enable students to identify ways that modern plays reflect the assumptions and convictions of the modern age

Notes to the Teacher

Modern drama, ranging from Ibsen and Chekhov through contemporary experimental forms, is characterized by enormous diversity. Lacking the long perspective that is available in considering Greek and Elizabethan drama, we find it much more difficult to distinguish significant from minor works and to capsulize the relationship between drama and culture. However, students have extensive experience with the attitudes, assumptions, and convictions of their culture. Thus, they are able to identify ways in which modern plays exhibit our world's diverse viewpoints and concerns.

Certainly, no exhaustive list of significant, serious modern drama is possible. However, a partial list of plays appropriate for study in an Advanced Placement class appears on page 94.

The lesson is intended to follow the study of conflict, characterization, theme, and theatrical elements in several modern plays. Sample answers for **Handout 31** are based on Ibsen's *A Doll's House*.

Procedure

1. Point out that just as Greek tragedy reflects the culture from which it emerged and Shakespearean drama mirrors many Elizabethan assumptions and convictions, so, too, modern drama mirrors the modern age.

2. Have students read and discuss page 1 of **Handout 31**. Emphasize that the list of key concepts is not exhaustive, but it does provide a place to start in describing a modern play's reflection of the modern age.

3. Have students use page 2 of the handout to probe some ways one of the modern plays they have read reflects the modern age. Encourage open-ended discussion, and allow for expression of each individual's viewpoints on the topic. Point out that characters, author, audience, and dominant culture may have contradictory viewpoints on a given subject; that, in itself, evidences something about our culture—the coexistence of diverse elements.

Suggested Responses:

God/Religion/The Supernatural

These are not mentioned in the play. There seems to be a basic assumption that religion is not necessarily a significant element in people's daily lives. This assumption also characterizes large segments of the modern world.

Men/Women

Roles and relationships of men and women are dominant concerns in the play. A Doll's House *questions the assumptions that women are inferior to men and that a woman's main responsibility is to care for family. These, too, are significant concerns in our modern world, but much change has occurred since Ibsen's day.*

Politics/Government

Politics and government are not directly dealt with in the play, but there is continuous awareness that breaking laws can have enormous consequences. The play mirrors a basic assumption that government seldom interferes with the lives of ordinary people. This is an assumption widely held in the United States, but one that not all nations equally cultivate.

Individual/Society

Nora's decision at the end of the play reflects the idea that each individual's primary responsibility is to self rather than to any other person or group. To the extent that we applaud her decision, we probably also endorse that emphasis on self-fulfillment.

Fate/Free Will

The characters in the play do make choices, and their choices have great consequences. Hence, the play seems to support the assumption that people may elect choices that profoundly shape the course of the future. People today have varying concepts of how fate and free will together affect lives.

Restraint/Indulgence

The play identifies restraint with strength, health, power, adulthood, masculinity; it links indulgence with weakness, femininity, childishness, illness. However, it also reverses these associations through Dr. Rank's restraint in announcing his impending death, Nora's emotional restraint near the end, and Torvald's self-indulged wrath.

Family

From the beginning of the play, the family is seen as a top priority by most of the characters. In the ensuing conflict, however, Torvald takes the position that family is secondary to absolute honor and integrity. Nora later sees individual self-development as a precondition for any capacity to make the family a real value. The family remains a troubled area in our modern world, and difficulties associated with family are related to the man/woman concept mentioned earlier.

4. Point out that this analytic process has equipped the class to write a critical essay relating a modern play to the modern age. Ask students to compose possible thesis statements for such a paper. Have them share their theses.

    Sample thesis: Henrik Ibsen's *A Doll's House* reflects the modern assumption that each individual's primary responsibility is personal development and fulfillment.

5. Direct each student to read a modern play, carefully consider its assumptions, convictions, and doubts, and write a paper relating these to the modern age.

Suggested list of modern dramas

Edward Albee
   Who's Afraid of Virginia Woolf
Maxwell Anderson
   Barefoot in Athens
Jean Anouilh
   Antigone
Samuel Beckett
   Waiting for Godot
Bertold Brecht
   Mother Courage
Anton Chekhov
   The Cherry Orchard
   Uncle Vanya
T. S. Eliot
   The Cocktail Party
Jean Giraudoux
   The Madwoman of Chaillot
Lillian Hellman
   The Children's Hour
   The Little Foxes
Henrick Ibsen
   A Doll's House
   Hedda Gabler
   The Wild Duck
Eugene Ionesco
   The Chairs
Federico Garcia Lorca
   Blood Wedding
Archibald MacLeish
   J. B.
Arthur Miller
   Death of a Salesman
   The Crucible
Eugene O'Neill
   The Hairy Ape
   A Long Day's Journey into Night
Harold Pinter
   The Birthday Party
Luigi Pirandello
   Henry IV
Jean-Paul Sartre
   No Exit
George Bernard Shaw
   Caesar and Cleopatra
   Saint Joan
   Pygmalion
John Millington Synge
   Riders to the Sea
Oscar Wilde
   The Importance of Being Earnest
Thornton Wilder
   Our Town
Tennessee Williams
   The Glass Menagerie
Paul Zindel
   The Effect of Gamma Rays on Man-in-the-Moon Marigolds

Modern Drama and the Modern Age

The long perspective of almost 2,500 years, with relatively few works and only three tragedians still extant, enables us to identify major movements, themes, and concerns of the Greek Golden Age and to relate them to classical tragedies. Similarly, 350 years provide a reasonable perspective on the genius of Shakespeare and the enormous vitality of the Elizabethan Age.

In considering modern drama, however, lack of sufficient perspective can make distinguishing major playwrights, plays, and cultural traits from tangential ones difficult. Therefore, our conclusions about modern drama's reflections of the modern age have a tentative quality.

Still, a play does mirror the convictions, assumptions, and doubts of the age and place from which it emerges. The play may endorse these attitudes; it may also cast doubt on some or all of them. Recognition of this interrelationship enriches understanding of the play itself and, perhaps more importantly, deepens insight into our own twentieth century.

Among topics to consider in analyzing a play's reflection of its age are
God/religion/the supernatural	science/technology
men/women	work/leisure
politics/government	fate/free will
economics	social equality/class distinctions
individual/society	integrity/opportunism
city/country	death/life
sickness/health	restraint/indulgence
war/peace	family
reality/illusion	alienation/isolation

In using these or other key concepts, ask yourself: What do the characters in the play say about this? What do they seem to think about it? Does the play as a whole support their viewpoints? How do these ideas reflect the time and place from which the play emerged? How do they reflect the spirit of our modern age?

Analysis of a Modern Play

Use any modern drama as a basis for identifying some assumptions, convictions, and/or doubts that characterize our society.

Title and author of play: _____

Key Concept	Evidence in Play	Basic Assumption, Conviction, or Doubt	Reflection of Contemporary Culture
God/Religion/ The Supernatural			
Men/Women			
Politics/Government			
Individual/Society			
Fate/Free Will			
Restraint/Indulgence			
Family			

Lesson 19
Timed Writing Assignments

Objective

- To provide students with practice in timed writings responding to dramatic passages

Notes to the Teacher

Advanced Placement essay questions used from 1970 to the present are available in packet form from College Board Publication Orders, Box 2815, Princeton, New Jersey 08540, at a reasonable cost.

The questions used in this lesson are patterned on the style of Advanced Placement questions in order to give your students an opportunity to work in this style as it pertains to a study of drama.

Procedure

1. Make sure students are supplied with sufficient writing materials. No student is to have access to books, papers, or notebooks during the timed writing experience. Try to avoid interruptions.

2. Distribute **Handout 32**, **33**, or **34**. Carefully observe time limits.

3. In grading these essays, you may want to use the Advanced Placement holistic method of scoring, which approximates the following guidelines:

Scores of 9–8
The essay is well-written and well-organized, indicating writer's superior capabilities in the process of analysis. The writer exhibits total understanding of question and response called for.

Scores of 7–6
The essay is less well-written and organized, perhaps not as structurally sound, but indicates writer's understanding of the demands of the question.

Score of 5
The essay is adequate in organization and structure, but may not offer sufficient support for analysis. The essay does not fully develop the response called for.

Scores of 4–3
The essay is inadequately written, with serious flaws in organization, perhaps coupled with some obvious misunderstanding of the question.

Score of 2
The essay is underdeveloped, poorly written, poorly organized, and includes only slight reference to the question.

Score of 1
The essay is too brief to be seriously considered and usually indicates total misconception of the question.

Timed Essay Question on Drama

Unlike the novelist, the playwright cannot include long passages of description but must often rely mainly on setting to provide information that adds a descriptive dimension to characters.

Select a play you have read in which this use of setting and its effect are evident. Write an essay in which you explain the author's technique in regard to setting. Do not give a plot summary.

You may write for forty minutes.

Name_____

Date _____

Timed Essay Question on Drama

Often the title of a play suggests its theme. Write an organized essay in which you explain this relationship of title to theme.

The titles given below are examples. You may choose one of these or another play of comparable literary merit.

A Doll's House	*Mourning Becomes Electra*	*The Taming of the Shrew*
The Glass Menagerie	*The Children's Hour*	*Who's Afraid of Virginia Woolf?*
An Enemy of the People	*No Exit*	*The Importance of Being Earnest*
Death of a Salesman	*The Effect of Gamma Rays on*	
The Wild Duck	*Man-in-the-Moon Marigolds*	

Do not write a summary of the plot. You may write for thirty minutes.

Name_____

Date _____

Timed Essay Question on Drama

The final scene in any drama is important to the resolution or lack of resolution of the work's conflict. In a well-organized essay, describe the final scene from a drama of literary merit, and show how it performs this function of closure. Be careful to avoid plot summary.

You may write for thirty-five minutes.

Lesson 20
The Novel: Its History and Types

Objective

- To acquaint students with background material about the novel as a literary genre

Notes to the Teacher

The following is prepared as a lecture on the novel. You may deliver the lecture in the usual way, or you may prefer to photocopy the material and distribute it as a handout.

The History of Novels

The novel as we know it had its origins in the classical storytelling literature of ancient Greece and Italy. By the end of the thirteenth century, A.D., the Italian novella was an established narrative form. As the popularity of this type of literature spread across the years and throughout Europe, it endured several influences but maintained its basic form. One of the major influences was contributed by Miguel de Cervantes in his *Don Quixote* in 1605.

The basic form is now defined as an extended prose narrative, but this is merely a skeletal definition. It has been fleshed out by the pioneering authors of 18th century England, including Daniel Defoe in his *Robinson Crusoe* in 1719 and *Moll Flanders* in 1722. Many texts cite Samuel Richardson's *Pamela*, written in 1740, as the first full-fledged novel in the English language. These early novels drew heavily upon the narrative qualities of their European predecessors.

Richardson's successful *Pamela* was followed with rapid development by Henry Fielding's *Joseph Andrews* in 1742 and *Tom Jones* in 1749. In 1748 Tobias Smollett had submitted *Roderick Random* for publication, adding to the growing appreciation of and demand for long narratives with character and plot development. So Defoe, Richardson, Fielding, and Smollett dropped the first pebbles into a pond, and the ripples have been widening ever since.

During the 1800s, the novel in the English language was expanded to incorporate American authors. James Fennimore Cooper's Leatherstocking series included *The Last of the Mohicans* in 1826 and *The Deerslayer*, in 1841. Nathaniel Hawthorne's masterpiece *The Scarlet Letter* was published in 1850 and remains a popular novel.

These successes were quickly followed by the publication of Herman Melville's *Moby Dick* in 1851, contemporary with Charlotte Brontë's *Jane Eyre* in 1847 and her sister Emily Brontë's *Wuthering Heights* written in 1848, on the other side of the Atlantic.

While America took time out to engage itself in a Civil War, England's writers continued to publish novels, establishing a period of Victorian prose. An abundance of social types along with increased complexity of plot action appeared in the novels of Charles Dickens, Anthony Trollope, and George Eliot. Thomas Hardy added a new direction called naturalism in his novels about the passionate lives of ordinary people, including *The Return of the Native* in 1878 and *Tess of the D'Urbervilles* in 1891.

American writers were quick to catch up with the opening of new frontiers following the Civil War. These writers created a style called realism. Leading writers included Stephen Crane, William Dean Howells, and Mark Twain. These realists depicted life and its struggles without glossing over the not-so-glamorous details.

With the dawn of the twentieth century, writers on both shores began to probe more deeply into the human mind. D. H. Lawrence's *Sons and Lovers*, Virginia Woolf's stream-of-consciousness style in *To the Lighthouse*, James Joyce's *Ulysses* and Theodore Dreiser's *An American Tragedy* turned readers' minds to introspection.

Two World Wars interrupted the output of novelists, but clustered around this period are writers such as Americans John Steinbeck, F. Scott Fitzgerald, Ernest Hemingway, and William Faulkner, who took the novel to newer and higher degrees of refinement.

The impact of global war and the resulting cultural changes sent novelists scattering into many different directions of thought. Disillusionment is a common theme in recent novels, as writers view their world with skepticism about the revolving-door values that engulf our society. Perhaps one of the few constants left is the novel itself, rich in its heritage and filled with unlimited potential as it enters stages of further development.

Procedure

1. Use information from Notes to the Teacher to acquaint students with the history of the novel.

2. Have students read **Handout 35** and discuss the varying types of novels. Point out that many novels can fit into more than one category.

3. Ask students to brainstorm titles of novels. Write the titles on the board, and ask students to categorize the novels as to type. Show how some novels represent more than one type.

Name_____

Date _____

Types of Novels

Type	Description	Examples
Picaresque	usually presents the life story of quick-witted rogues and their adventures in an episodic style	*Moll Flanders* *Don Quixote*
Gothic	combines a desolate setting and mysterious events to create an atmosphere of terror	*Castle of Otrano* *Frankenstein*
Gothic Romance	presents a stormy love relationship within a violent, brooding atmosphere	*Jane Eyre* *Wuthering Heights* *Rebecca*
Novel of Manners	defines social mores of a specific group, often the upper-middle class, which controls the actions of the characters	*Pride and Prejudice*
Satirical	reveals human folly and vices through wit, scorn, ridicule, and exaggeration, with hope for reform	*Animal Farm* *The Loved One* *Brideshead Revisited*
Realistic	portrays life objectively, without idealization; reveals unpleasantness	*Sister Carrie* *Jude the Obscure* *The Red Badge of Courage*
Naturalistic	pessimistically portrays sordidness, squalor, and violence through characters who have no control over their destinies	*American Tragedy* *Maggie, A Girl of the Streets* *Nana*
Sociological	depicts the problems and injustices of society; makes moral judgments and offers resolution	*The Grapes of Wrath* *Lords of the Flies* *To Kill a Mockingbird* *Cry, the Beloved Country*
Psychological	emphasizes internal motives, conflicts, opinions of main characters, which then develop the external action	*The Stranger* *The Catcher in the Rye* *Siddhartha*
Historical	centers on individuals, society, or events from the past, combined with fictional characterizations	*Kenilworth* *A Tale of Two Cities* *The Source*
Science Fiction	imagines the impact of real or hypothetical scientific developments on individuals or society	*1984* *On the Beach* *Farenheit 451* *Stranger in a Strange Land*
Regional Novel	represents accurately the habits, speech, and folklore of a particular geographical section	*The Return of the Native* *Huckleberry Finn*
Stream-of-Consciousness	presents the total range of thoughts, memories, associations of a character in uninterrupted, endless flow	*Ulysses* *Mrs. Dalloway* *As I Lay Dying*

Lesson 21
Point of View in the Novel

Objectives

- To enable students to recognize the author's point of view in a narrative
- To sensitize students to the contribution of the author's style to point of view

Notes to the Teacher

One of the most difficult concepts for the student to understand and use is point of view, which is to narrative prose what tone is to expository prose or poetry. This concept has become increasingly important and more complex as novelists have grown more interested in psychological relationships and the relativity of perceptions.

In modern novels, the omniscient author who makes moral pronouncements to "Dear Reader" has, for the most part, given way to the author's persona, a created character through whom all perceptions in the novel are filtered, perhaps even through a stream of consciousness technique. In between these two kinds of point of view remains the objective viewpoint, scrupulously careful not only to report events but also to avoid commenting on them. One of the most important single decisions an author makes in writing is the choice of the point of view from which to tell the story.

The establishment of a point of view depends most importantly on two other elements of the novel: style and structure. This lesson is devoted to an examination of the different points of view and how style is used to develop them. In the next lesson, we will return to point of view to show how it is reinforced by structure.

One distinction that may aid students is that point of view has nothing to do with the content of a passage. It is concerned solely with the technique by which material is presented. If the analogy of a photograph is used, point of view designates not picture content but camera angle.

After several passages are examined to distinguish various types of point of view, two episodes from James Joyce's *A Portrait of the Artist as a Young Man* are compared to show how point of view is manipulated by a master. Joyce's point of view is influenced strongly by his Irish Catholicism, against which he rebelled but to which he was indebted for imagery and symbolism, even as he wrote of leaving his church and country.

Procedure

1. Write the following role-play prompts on four 3×5 cards. Ask four students to argue their points of view before the class. Have each student present his or her entire case before the next student speaks. When all four have finished, lead a class discussion on how point of view is established. Concepts that may be considered include establishing a point of view through

   a. selection of only certain facts to discuss

   b. use of emotionally loaded language

   c. individualized interpretation of events

   Role-play prompts

   Card 1 You are a high school student who has been sent to the principal's office by your teacher for being late to class for the third time. Argue that you should not be sent to detention hall.

   Card 2 You are a high school teacher who has sent one of your students to the principal for being late to class three times. This student has given you trouble by being discourteous, and you want the student sent to detention hall. Argue your case before the principal.

   Card 3 You are a minister who believes only God has the right to take a life. Argue against capital punishment in a Sunday sermon.

   Card 4 You are a convicted murderer on Death Row. Argue against capital punishment as you talk to a newspaper reporter who has come for an interview.

2. Distribute **Handout 36,** and ask students to read it. Develop inductively from the passages read the differences between the three major types of point of view. Identification of the point of view of each passage is as follows:

Passage 1—*third person, limited*

Passage 2—*third person, objective*

Passage 3—*third person, multiple consciousness*

Passage 4—*third person, omniscient*

3. Have students use **Handout 37** to expand their understanding of point of view.

4. Distribute **Handout 38,** and ask students to read it. Explain that Joyce uses a developing point of view in order to show his protagonist's responses rather than tell about them. The reader of this novel is held within the consciousness of young Stephen Daedalus, who grows during the period of the book from about age two to about age twenty. (Since the novel has very few references to Stephen's exact age, these ages are approximate.) Joyce has identified nineteen different moments or "presents" that impinge upon Stephen's consciousness during those years. Through differentiating styles, the words and syntax through which Stephen thinks, Joyce makes the reader aware not only of what Stephen apprehends but also of how Stephen apprehends.

Ask students to compare the two passages to distinguish between the nine-year-old point of view and the seventeen-year-old point of view. Use the following questions to conduct class discussion.

a. What are Stephen's differing concerns underlying each passage?

At nine, Stephen is single-mindedly focused on his unjust punishment. Childishness is evident in "his prayer to be let off" (l.10); his attempt to keep from crying (l.11); his shame when he does cry (l.19 and 24).

At seventeen, Stephen has grown in self-confidence to the point that he is happy to be alone and "unheeded." His response to the bird-girl reveals his past lust and the guilt he felt over it: though she has a beautiful female form (her thighs, breasts, and hair are carefully described), she is pure. His religious tendencies are shown through religious imagery (dove, flame, "sign upon the flesh" [l.10]), and Stephen's reactions ("worship" [l.18] and "Heavenly God!" [l.26]).

b. How do figures of speech show Stephen's increased maturity, as well as Joyce's attitude toward the event described?

At nine, Stephen compares the sound of the pandy bat to "the loud crack of a broken stick," (l.5) a commonplace though effective simile. He compares his hurt hands to "a leaf in the fire" (l.6) and "a loose leaf in the air" (l.9), the repetition showing his relatively simplistic thinking.

At seventeen, Stephen has the girl at the shore in the likeness of a bird, a suitable mate-muse for him since he hopes to fly the heights of poetic inspiration. The metaphor is beautifully worked out in careful detail ("legs delicate as crane's," "featherings of soft down" "dovetailed behind her," "bosom was as a bird's," "as the breast of some darkplumaged dove"). The added significance of associating the girl with a saint ("a sign upon the flesh"), with a dove (often the symbol of the Holy Spirit), and finally with a flame (often symbolizing God's presence) is reinforced by Stephen's exclamation, "Heavenly God!" and his "profane joy," which Joyce means us to take as, in fact, sanctified. Stephen's calling to be an artist, of which this scene is a part, is surely God-directed, as seen by the interlocking religious figures in this passage.

c. How does the syntax in each passage reflect the maturing mind of Stephen?

At nine, Stephen overuses the conjunction "and" to string his sentences together.

At seventeen, Stephen's sentences are much more varied in length (from three to forty-six words in paragraph 1). His first sentence of only three words carries a strong emphasis. The usual grammatical order is sometimes violated for emphasis: l.16 "her face" and l.19 "long, long." There is a marked rhythmical flow to the prose.

108

d. How does the diction show the difference in Stephen's maturity?

At nine, Stephen's artistic bent is shown by his use of adjective series that have sound repetitions: l.5 "burning stinging tingling blow"; l.16–17 "maddening tingling burning pain." The actual repetitions of words here, as elsewhere, again show the nine-year-old's limited vocabulary.

At seventeen, Stephen's prose is almost poetic. The repetition of "hither and thither" have a lulling, soothing effect. The words and their arrangement in l.16 reinforce the sense of wonder. The mood of quiet reverence is reinforced by diction in many places.

Varieties of Points of View

Passage 1

She began to enjoy sitting on the porch with him, but she could never tell if he knew she was there or not. Even when he answered her, she couldn't tell if he knew it was she. She herself. Mrs. Flood, the landlady. Not just anybody. They would sit, he only sit, and she sit rocking, for half an afternoon and not two words seemed to pass between them, though she might talk at length. If she didn't talk and keep her mind going, she would find herself sitting forward in her chair, looking at him with her mouth not closed. Anyone who saw her from the sidewalk would think she was being courted by a corpse.

From Wise Blood, Flannery O' Conner

Passage 2

Ma set her lantern on the floor. She reached behind one of the boxes that had served as chairs and brought out a stationery box, old and soiled and cracked at the corners. She sat down and opened the box. Inside were letters, clippings, photographs, a pair of earrings, a little gold signet ring, and a watch chain braided of hair and tipped with gold swivels. She touched the letters with her fingers, touched them lightly, and she smoothed a newspaper clipping on which there was an account of Tom's trial. For a long time she held the box, looking over it, and her fingers disturbed the letters and then lined them up again. She bit her lower lip, thinking, remembering. And at last she made up her mind. She picked out the ring, the watch charm, the earrings, dug under the pile and found one gold cuff link. She took a letter from an envelope and dropped the trinkets in the envelope. She folded the envelope over and put it in her dress pocket. Then gently and tenderly she closed the box and smoothed the top carefully with her fingers. Her lips parted. And then she stood up, took her lantern, and went back into the kitchen. She lifted the stove lid and laid the box gently among the coals. Quickly the heat browned the paper. A flame licked up and over the box. She replaced the stove lid and instantly the fire sighed up and breathed over the box.

From The Grapes of Wrath, John Steinbeck

Passage 3

. . . she had known happiness, exquisite happiness, intense happiness, and it silvered the rough waves a little more brightly, as daylight faded, and the blue went out of the sea and it rolled in waves of pure lemon which curved and swelled and broke upon the beach and the ecstasy burst in her eyes and waves of pure delight raced over the floor of her mind and she felt, it is enough! It is enough!

He turned and saw her. Ah! She was lovely, lovelier now than ever he thought. But he could not speak to her. He could not interrupt her. He wanted urgently to speak to her now that James was gone and she was alone at last. But he resolved, no; he would not interrupt her. She was aloof from him now in her beauty, in her sadness. He would let her be, and he passed her without a word, though it hurt him that she should look so distant, and he could not reach her, he could do nothing to help her. And again he could have passed her without a word had she not, at that very moment, given him of her own free will what she knew he would never ask, and called to him and taken the green shawl off the picture frame, and gone to him. For he wished, she knew, to protect her.

From To the Lighthouse, Virginia Woolf

Passage 4

Happy for all her maternal feelings was the day on which Mrs. Bennet got rid of her two most deserving daughters. With what delighted pride she afterwards visited Mrs. Bingley, and talked of Mrs. Darcy, may be guessed. I wish I could say, for the sake of her family, that the accomplishment of her earnest desire in the establishment of so many of her children produced so happy an effect as to make her a sensible, amiable, well-informed woman for the rest of her life; though, prehaps, it was luck for her husband, who might not have relished domestic felicity in so unusual a form, that she still was occasionally nervous, and invariably silly.

From *Pride and Prejudice*, Jane Austen

Point of View

General Questions

1. Is the author sympathetic or unsympathetic with the narrator?

2. How does the point of view enhance the story's theme?

Types of Point of View

1. Third person, objective—No thoughts or feelings of characters are recorded. The narrator becomes a camera, recording actions and behaviors without comment or interpretation. This narrator cannot record thoughts or feelings. Readers must read between the lines to discover the tone and thoughts behind the words.

2. Third person, omniscient—The all-knowing consciousness. The following are indications of omniscience (in increasingly intrusive order):

   a. Thoughts, feelings, perceptions of characters reported as narrator, not character, understands them

   b. Setting descriptions that do not arise from character's actions

   c. Identifications of characters on first appearance—introductions

   d. Temporal summaries (what happened before or after)

   e. Summary that epitomizes a character or event

   f. Commentary from the narrator

      1. Explicit commentary

         a. Interpretation—to explain the relevance or significance of an event or reaction

         b. Judgment—to evaluate on the basis of certain criteria held by the narrator

         c. Generalization—to apply significance from the narrative to the wider world

         d. Self-conscious narration—comments on the narrative itself

      2. Implicit commentary or ironic narration—Narrator is conscious of and intends irony; the butt of the irony is the character(s) or society described.

3. Third person, limited omniscient—Narrator's knowledge of thoughts, actions, visual perceptions, and feelings is limited to one of a few characters.

4. First person—Point of view is limited to the consciousness of a particular character(s). Indications of subjective viewpoint

   a. Thoughts, feelings, and perceptions of the narrating character who refers to himself or herself as "I" are reported as they seem to that character, happening now. Focus is not only on the action but also on what the narrator makes of it.

   b. Other characters (what they look like, what they do, what they think) appear only through the narrator's consciousness.

Narrative Framework

1. Without frame—Events are reported as though they were happening just as the reader reads about them.

2. With frame—Narrator appears at beginning and usually at end of narrative to tell his or her story to listener(s) outside the main narrative.

Narrator's Reliability

1. Author's attitude toward narrator

   a. Reliable—Narrator is a trustworthy, intelligent, insightful, involved, and knowledgeable guide.

   b. Reliable/unreliable—Narrator has limited capacities because of

      1. Tunnel vision—Narrator sees only one type of thing.

      2. Confused emotions—Narrator's involvement keeps him or her from being an accurate reporter.

      3. Naivete—Narrator is incapable of understanding what he or she reports.

   c. Unreliable—Narrator is dishonest to make him or herself look good.

   d. Unreliable—Narrator is a pawn of the author, i.e., manipulated to withhold information to provide suspense (detective story, Saki's stories).

2. Reader's detection of narrator's unreliability through inconsistencies in narrator's story

   a. Narrator has invalid presuppositions that distort his or her view.

   b. Narrator does not suppress certain facts that, when reported to the reader, are inconsistent with the narrator's conclusions.

Two Passages from *A Portrait of the Artist as a Young Man*

Passage 1

When Stephen Is about Nine

Stephen closed his eyes and held out in the air his trembling hand with the palm upwards. He felt the prefect of studies touch it for a moment in the fingers to straighten it and then the swish of the sleeve of the soutane as the pandy bat was lifted to strike. A hot burning stinging tingling blow like the loud crack of a broken stick made his trembling hand crumple together like a leaf in the fire: and at the sound and the pain scalding tears were driven into his eyes. His whole body was shaking with fright, his arm was shaking and his crumpled burning livid hand shook like a loose leaf in the air. A cry sprang to his lips, a prayer to be let off. But though the tear scalded his eyes and his limbs quivered with pain and fright he held back the hot tears and the cry that scalded his throat.—Other hand! shouted the prefect of studies.

Stephen drew back his maimed and quivering right arm and held out his left hand. The soutane sleeve swished again as the pandy bat was lifted and a loud crashing sound and a fierce maddening tingling, burning pain made his hand shrink together with the palms and fingers in a livid quivering mass. The scalding water burst forth from his eyes and, burning with shame and agony and fear, he drew back his shaking arm in terror and burst out into a whine of pain. His body shook with a palsy of fright and in shame and rage he felt the scalding cry come from his throat and the scalding tears falling out of his eyes and down his flaming cheeks.—Kneel down! cried the prefect of studies.

Stephen knelt down quickly pressing his beaten hands to his sides. To think of them beaten and swollen with pain all in a moment made him feel so sorry for them as if they were not his own but someone else's that he felt sorry for.

From *A Portrait of the Artist as a Young Man*, James Joyce

Passage 2

When Stephen Is about Seventeen

He was alone. He was unheeded, happy and near to the wild heart of life. He was alone and young and willful and wildhearted, alone amid a waste of wild air and brackish waters and the seaharvest of shells and tangle and veiled grey sunlight and gayclad lightclad figures, of children and girls and voices childish and girlish in the air.

A girl stood before him in midstream, alone and still, gazing out to sea. She seemed like one whom magic had changed into the likeness of a strange and beautiful seabird. Her long slender bare legs were delicate as a crane's and pure save where an emerald trail of seaweed had fashioned itself as a sign upon the flesh. Her thighs, fuller and softhued as ivory, were bared almost to the hips where the white fringes of her drawers were like featherings of soft white down. Her slateblue skirts were kilted boldly about her waist and dovetailed behind her. Her bosom was as a bird's soft and slight, slight and soft as the breast of some darkplumaged dove. But her long fair hair was girlish: and girlish, and touched with the wonder of mortal beauty, her face.

She was alone and still, gazing out to sea; and when she felt his presence and the worship of his eyes her eyes turned to him in quiet sufferance of his gaze, without shame or wantonness. Long, long she suffered his gaze and then quietly withdrew her eyes from his and bent them towards the stream, gently stirring the water with her foot hither and thither. The first faint noise of gently moving water broke the silence, low and faint and whispering, faint as the bells of sleep; hither and thither, hither and thither: and a faint flame trembled on her cheek.—Heavenly God! cried Stephen's soul, in an outburst of profane joy.

From *A Portrait of the Artist as a Young Man*, James Joyce

Lesson 22
Structural Organization in the Novel

- To give students five approaches to the structural analysis of novels

Notes to the Teacher

Since the novel is such a massive piece of literature, it is often hard for students to see its underlying structure. This lesson explores five approaches to the structure of a novel. Again, some of these approaches will be more appropriate and useful than others for any particular novel. Students should be advised to choose two or three approaches for their novel.

Procedure

1. Write on the board the word *skeleton*. Brainstorm with students the functions of a skeleton. Focus on the skeleton's structural functions as a framework to hold the body together, to hold a building together or (a skeleton outline) to hold a composition together. Remind them that the length of a novel makes seeing the novel's skeleton very difficult, but emphasize that this lesson is an attempt to help them clarify that concept and its applications. You may want to remind them of Aristotle's unity of action (which provided such a tight structure for Greek tragedy) and of the work on structure they have already done in their analysis of the unity of action in *Oedipus*.

2. Have students read **Handout 39** and apply the five types to novels the class has read together.

3. Have students apply the theory to an additional novel individually, by groups, or by the class as a whole.

4. Ask students to write papers analyzing the structure of a novel.

Approaches to Analyze Structural Unity in the Novel

Each of the following approaches to analyzing the structure of a novel is useful for some novels but not equally useful for every novel. As you examine a particular novel, select the two or three approaches that are most helpful. For each approach, ask the following central question: What is the logic behind this arrangement of materials?

Note that some novels, particularly earlier ones, are not tightly structured. The picaresque novel, for example, consists of a series of loosely organized episodes centering around a hero's experiences. The arrangement of the episodes may or may not be important. *Don Quixote* and *The Adventures of Huckleberry Finn* are two novels of this type.

Approach 1 **Structural Divisions**

A novel is usually divided into chapters or parts, often according to a structural design. If characters and setting change from one chapter or part to another, it is worthwhile to try to find a logical reason for the division made by the author. Sometimes such divisions will coincide with geographical settings and character involvement, as in *Madame Bovary*, where the action of the first section originates in the convent, where Emma dreams dreams that seem to be fulfilled by Charles, whom she marries. The action for section two originates at LaVaubyessard, where Emma gets her first taste of aristocratic life, making her ready for her affair with Rodolphe. The action of section three originates in Rouen at the opera, where the romantic life of the heroine and the appearance of the star prepare her for romance with Leon.

Approach 2 **Polarization of Characters**

Since the novelist must simplify life's complexities, and since the novelist wishes to convey an idea, the novelist usually lines up characters so that they represent polarized values or attitudes toward life. In this way, as in the short story, the writer is able to point to a truth that is revealed through the way the conflict between the characters is resolved. Such polarization of characters is most easily seen in novels where there is an obvious external conflict, such as *A Passage to India* or *Lord of the Flies*. In *A Passage to India*, characters either believe in the innocence of Assiz or in his guilt (perhaps displaying a cultural bias against Indian moslems). In *Lord of the Flies*, characters either side with Jack, the brutal dictator, or with Ralph, the rational democrat. In many novels where the conflict is less obvious, characterization is nonetheless polarized. In *Return of the Native*, characters are divided between those who are at peace on the heath, such as Clym and the reddleman, and those who fight it, such as Eustacia.

Approach 3 **Repetition of Patterns or Elements**

As in all literary analysis, students of the novel should be alert to any repetition of elements such as images, symbols, conflicts, or characterization. Subplots in a novel often provide another look at the central character's problem, either by paralleling or contrasting character traits or situations. Symbolic patterns help structure many novels. Two novels that make very effective use of religious symbolism are *The Brothers Karamazov*, in which the fatherhood of God is examined through the relationships between fathers and sons in the novel, and *Light in August*, in which Joe Christmas is an inverted Christ figure. The two central characters in *Wise Blood* develop in directly opposite ways. Hazel Motes develops from a man fearful of dying and going to hell because of his sin to a man who has accepted his sinful nature and has done an extreme penance for it, who has (in terms of fundamentalist Christianity) against his will been saved by the "wise blood" of Christ. On the other hand, Enoch Emery, who trusts in his own wise blood, and acts unthinkingly according to his instincts, reverts to an animal-existence in which he is happy inside a gorilla suit as he tries to shake hands with everyone as did his model, Gonga the ape. Structurally, this novel can be diagrammed by an X: Enoch begins at the level of a man and descends to an ape, while Hazel begins at the level of a man and ascends to a saint.

Approach 4 **Resolution of Conflict**

As in the short story, the resolution of conflict is a key element in setting the thematic emphasis of the novel. The resolution should be examined to discover its implications for the protagonist, for the society of the novel, and for life in general. Exploring how the resolution of the novel is appropriate for the entire work is important. Readers may want to examine a resolution that was considered but rejected by the author, such as Raskolnikov's suicide at the end of *Crime and Punishment*, to determine why the author made the decision to end the novel differently. Sometimes the resolution may give a clear indication of the author's intent but still raise questions about how consistent it is with the logic of the novel. In *Sons and Lovers*, Paul's central problem is his Oedipal fixation upon his mother that makes him unable to relate completely to either of his two lovers. At the end of the novel, Paul's mother dies of cancer, aided by an overdose of painkiller from Paul. Having broken off from both his women, Paul considers suicide but instead quickly walks toward the brightly lighted town. The reader understands Lawrence's symbolism to mean that Paul has shaken off the psychological hold his mother has had upon him and is now ready to find a woman to whom he can relate completely. However, such an easy resolution of such a difficult problem may not be convincing to all readers.

Approach 5 **Narrative Point of View**

An analysis of point of view should examine the function of the frame, if present: it may establish the narrator as moral evaluator of the action to follow, as in *The Great Gatsby* or in the novels of Conrad where Marlowe serves as narrator. The frame may simply provide a context that reveals the ultimate resolution or lack of it, as in *The Catcher in the Rye*, where the frame closure reveals that Holden is telling his story from a psychiatric ward. The unreliability of the narrator may provide ambiguity of meaning for the whole narrative, as in *Turn of the Screw*, which critics still cannot agree upon. The involvement of the author with the reader so that the narrator's words are directed ultimately at the reader in an attempt to have the reader discover something about his or her own values occurs in both *The Secret Sharer* and *Heart of Darkness*, where Conrad hopes that through identification with the narrator the reader will discover his or her own dark side. Point of view to gain narrator-reader identification is used in a different way but for a similar didactic purpose in Camus's *The Fall*, which is written entirely as a monologue-confession, deliberately designed to get the reader, as well as the unheard listener, to confess his or her own egotism to the narrator, who can thus feel superior.

Lesson 23
Discussion Approaches

Objective

- To provide students with thought-provoking discussion approaches that will enhance their appreciation of the novel

Notes to the Teacher

Because Advanced Placement classes are generally composed of highly capable and motivated students, the exchange of ideas in discussion is often the most effective tool for increasing each individual's sensitivity to theme, style, structure, and other literary elements. However, overuse of the question-answer format can dull enthusiasm. This lesson is intended to provide several alternative discussion approaches to spice up classroom exchange about novels.

Procedure

Approach 1

1. Have students work in pairs or small groups to write a short statement expressing their most profound insight into the novel to be discussed.
2. Have the whole class sit in a large circle.
3. Ask one volunteer to read a statement.
4. Allow other students from the same group to make comments that help clarify that statement. (Note that only clarifying comments are admissible at this time.)
5. Ask all class members to write two or three questions that would help to probe the group's position.
6. In the next part of the discussion, class members direct their questions to the group. (Note that the class may only pose questions, whereas the group members try to answer them.)
7. Have group members summarize ways in which the class has helped to refine their perceptions.
8. Repeat the same process, using the statement of another group.

Approach 2

1. Ask one student to adopt the identity of one character in the novel.
2. Invite other students to ask questions about that character's actions, motives, and feelings.
3. The student-characters must try to give correct answers from the novel; if correct answers are not known, the student-character must bluff.
4. All other students record wrong or bluffed answers.
5. After ten minutes, have students compare lists of wrong or bluffed answers.

Approach 3

1. Pretend to be the author of the novel, or have a student who has read background information pretend to be the author.
2. Have students ask questions about the plot, characters, details, theme, style, or any other aspect of the novel.
3. Ask students to spot and challenge incorrect or invented answers.

Approach 4

1. Have students, working in small groups, adopt the roles of characters in the novel years after the end of the novel.
2. Have them prepare to role-play characters' conversations in which they reminisce and reflect upon the events in the novel.
3. Have groups present role-played conversations.

Approach 5

1. Diagram Erikson's stages of human development, Kohlberg's theory of moral development, Maslow's theory, or any other stage theory of human growth.
2. Have students use these stages to analyze the major characters and their actions, motives, and feelings.

Approach 6

1. Assign each student the role of a character from the novel.

2. Direct students to pretend that their characters have been invited to speak to the class to give two or three minutes of advice on the basis of personal experiences in the novel.

3. Allow students time to prepare comments.

4. Have each student deliver the character's comments to the class.

Lesson 24
Timed Writings on Novels

Objective

- To increase each student's ability to analyze, organize, and compose quickly and effectively

Notes to the Teacher

As with other genres, the novel can be explored with a wide variety of impromptu essay topics. These not only help prepare students for the Advanced Placement examination but also help students to become more efficient in analyzing literature, organizing concepts, and writing effective compositions. The exercises included here may be used as Advanced Placement practice work or adapted for tests on specific novels.

Procedure

1. Distribute **Handout 40**, **41**, **42**, or **43**, and allow students thirty-five minutes to complete essays.

2. Make copies or transparencies of several students' essays, and conduct in-class evaluations. (Note comments in Lessons 15 and 19.) The following are some general comments regarding responses to these timed writings. Point out the limits of the question that you assigned, and caution students that sometimes they make serious mistakes by answering a question on a significant novel with an essay about a drama, such as *Hamlet*, or about light fiction, such as *Jaws*.

Handout 40

Novel chosen should be written in first person; the answer will probably be more effective if the narrator's reliability is limited, for example, as in *Great Expectations* or *A Separate Peace*. Specific examples of any instances when the narrator's judgments are not reliable should be included.

Handout 41

This essay should include accurate identification of external and internal conflicts, recognition of the conflicts' outcomes, and a clear explanation of cause-effect relationships among the conflicts. Among the many appropriate novel selections are *The Power and the Glory* and *The Scarlet Letter*.

Handout 42

This question can be applied to many novels, among them *Anna Karenina* and *The Sound and the Fury*. The essay should include an accurate account of the opening pages and clear establishment of theme connections.

Handout 43

Among effective selections for this question could be *Wise Blood*, *Don Quixote*, and *The Adventures of Huckleberry Finn*. Essay should include clear treatments of paradox, irony, wisdom, foolishness, the "wise fool," and the "foolish sage."

Timed Essay Question on the Novel

The reader's understanding of events, characters, and themes in first person narration is sifted through the narrator's perceptions. Comprehension of the work thus necessitates an accurate assessment of the reliability of the narrator—the speaker's honesty, intelligence, insight, involvement, pride, and knowledge, for example. Show how this assessment can affect one's reading of one specific novel of recognized literary merit.

You may write for thirty-five minutes.

Name_____

Date _____

Timed Essay Question on the Novel

In many novels, the protagonist experiences simultaneous internal and external conflicts. Often the external conflicts catalyze the internal ones, which in the end emerge as most important. Show how this is true in any one novel of generally recognized literary merit.

You may write for thirty-five minutes.

Timed Essay Question on the Novel

Close examination of the opening pages of a novel often reveals the themes that dominate the work as a whole. Show how this is true of any one novel of established literary merit.

You may write for thirty-five minutes.

Name_____

Date _____

Timed Essay Question on the Novel

The paradoxical and ironic relationships between wisdom and foolishness, sometimes typified by the relationship between a king and a court jester, are evident in many great works of literature. Show how this is true of any one novel of established literary merit.

You may write for thirty-five minutes.

Part 2
Synthesis

Once students have acquired analytic skills, they are ready to move beyond analysis to the exciting arena of synthesis. Organized thematically, this part of the unit provides materials to help you and your students cross-relate poems, stories, plays, novels, and nonfiction dealing with similar topics.

The first section focuses on human aspirations to greatness. A variety of literary works prompt students to explore people's experiences with ambition, leadership, arrogance, exploitation, sloth, dignity, and fate.

The ageless yearning to love and be loved has captured the imaginations of writers throughout the centuries. In the second section, students consider the paradoxes, ironies, and demands of love commitments, as evidenced in a variety of literary works.

Social responsibility is the topic of the lessons in the third section. Students probe literary treatments of two major social concerns: war and oppression of minorities.

Finally, the fourth section provides materials for an intensive approach to reality and illusion as a dominant literary motif. A variety of works catalyze exploration of people's desire and need for truth, as well as their simultaneous desire and need for illusions.

Lesson 25

Four Poems about Human Aspirations to Greatness

Objective

- To have students compare and contrast several literary views of human aspirations to greatness

Notes to the Teacher

The human potential for greatness, along with the potential for evil and foolishness, has concerned writers and thinkers throughout history. These views of humanity's aspirations and possibilities are central to the great traditions of comedy and tragedy; they are also key factors in epics, narrative poems, drama, fiction, and biography. Various works illustrate multiple facts: the admirably great human being, who is true to self and others; the person whose aspirations outstrip capability, leading to failure; the person whose potential is stifled by fear, sloth, or greed; the person whose ambitions lead to cruelty and injustice; the person whose aspirations seem somehow fated to failure.

In this lesson, students relate four poems to the logic of human potential. They then synthesize their understanding by cross-relating the poems.

Procedure

1. Conduct a brief discussion of human greatness by asking students:

    a. What does it mean to be a great person?

    b. Who are some people that you would describe as great?

    c. Who are some people that many people consider great?

    d. What makes any given individual strive to be great?

    e. Why doesn't everyone aim for greatness?

    f. Why doesn't everyone who strives for greatness reach greatness?

2. Point out that writers of all ages have concerned themselves with these and other questions about the human potential for greatness.

3. Have students read **Handout 44**. Point out that "Ulysses" is another name for Odysseus, the wily hero of the great Greek epic, *The Odyssey*. Then ask students to answer the questions on the handout.

4. Review responses.

    Suggested Responses:

    1. *Old, impatient with his situation; eager for knowledge, adventure, and life; strong and optimistic; a leader*

    2. *"To follow knowledge with a sinking star, Beyond the utmost bound of human thought."*

        ". . . something ere the end, Some work of noble note, may yet be done . . ."

        "Come, my friends, 'Tis not too late to seek a newer world."

        ". . . that which we are, we are: One equal temper of heroic hearts, Made weak by time and fate, but strong in will To strive, to seek, to find, and not to yield."

    3. *People who respond to a challenge, who share his desire to pursue an active and searching life, who are daring and optimistic*

    4. *Tennyson seems to be promoting human aspirations to greatness. The poem encourages us to adopt Ulysses' philosophy of life.*

5. Have students read **Handout 45** and complete the exercise.

6. Review responses.

Suggested Responses:

1. *Both are impatient with their current situations, and both long for adventure and glory. However, Miniver is focused on passively thinking about his situation, while Ulysses is a man of action. Ulysses prompts our admiration, while Miniver evokes our pity and, perhaps, scorn.*

2. *Robinson's ironic description of Miniver emphasizes that idle dreaming is not a path to greatness. Miniver needs more than signs, regrets, and another drink if he really wants glory and adventure.*

7. Have students read **Handout 46** and answer the questions.

8. Review responses.

Suggested Responses:

1. *The inscription proclaims Ozymandias' pride in the glory and magnitude of his accomplishments.*

2. *The irony lies in the contrast between these haughty words and the "colossal wreck" of the statue.*

3. *The poem implies that human accomplishments, like people themselves, are transitory.*

9. Have students read **Handout 47**. Point out that Tolstoy was the great Russian author of *Anna Karenina* and *War and Peace*. Esenin, Mayakovsky, Gorky, and Pasternak were also significant Russian writers. Ask students the following questions.

   a. Who is Hemingway?

   a significant twentieth-century American writer

   b. Who is the victim of "The Dallas Whaler/ With a Telescopic Sight"?

   U.S. President John Fitzgerald Kennedy

   c. What lines help to clarify for you the theme of this poem?

   "Enormity commands everyone/to hunt for it." ". . . greatness is helpless." "Greatness kills greatness." "A big drive is on;/ we cherish their names posthumously." ". . . white men have a funny custom:/ After planting the harpoon,/they weep over the corpse."

10. Point out that Yevtushenko, like Tennyson, Robinson, and Shelley, is dealing with human greatness. Ask students to answer the question on **Handout 47**.

11. Review responses.

Suggested Response:

Yevtushenko points out that people tend to try to destroy others who become great. Yet, at the same time that they persecute the great person, people also admire him or her; once the persecution succeeds, this admiration is expressed through mourning and eulogies.

12. Point out that after reading these four poems we emerge with a new understanding of the Romantic concern, "human aspirations to greatness." Ask students to write a short paragraph describing their new understanding. Then have volunteers share and comment on their insights.

Example:
These four poems reveal the paradoxes of human aspirations to greatness. It is evident that productive living requires a Ulysses-like approach to life and that Miniver's escapism is futile. Yet, it is also clear that Ulysses, despite his stirring philosophy and enthusiasm, is as transitory as Ozymandias. Like the whales in Yevtushenko's poem, Ulysses, too, in achieving greatness, will undoubtedly invite the persecutions of others of "a savage race."

132

Ulysses

It little profits that an idle king,
By this still hearth, among these barren crags,
Matched with an aged wife, I mete and dole
Unequal laws into a savage race,
That hoard, and sleep, and feed, and know not me.
I cannot rest from travel; I will drink
Life to the lees. All times I have enjoyed
Greatly, have suffered greatly, both with those
That loved me, and alone; on shore, and when
Through scudding drifts the rainy Hyades
Vext the dim sea. I am become a name;
For always roaming with a hungry heart
Much have I seen and known,—cities of men
And manners, climates, councils, governments,
Myself not least, but honored of them all;
And drunk delight of battle with my peers,
Far on the ringing plains of windy Troy.
I am a part of all that I have met;
Yet all experience is an arch where through
Gleams that untraveled world, whose margin fades.
For ever and for ever when I move.
How dull it is to pause, to make an end,
To rust unburnished, not to shine in use!
As though to breathe were life! Life piled on life
Were all too little, and of one to me
Little remains; but every hour is saved
From that eternal silence, something more,
A bringer of new things; and vile it were
For some three suns to store and hoard myself,
And this grey spirit yearning in desire
To follow knowledge like a sinking star,
Beyond the utmost bound of human thought.

This is my son, mine own Telemachus,
To whom I leave the scepter and the isle—
Well-loved of me, discerning to fulfill
This labor, by slow prudence to make mild
A rugged people, and through soft degrees
Subdue them to the useful and the good.
Most blameless is he, centered in the sphere
Of common duties, decent not to fail
In offices of tenderness, and pay
Meet adoration to my household gods,
When I am gone. He works his work, I mine.

There lies the port; the vessel puffs her sail:
There gloom the dark, broad seas. My mariners,
Souls that have toiled, and wrought, and thought with me—
That ever with frolic welcome took
The thunder and the sunshine and opposed
Free hearts, free foreheads—you and I are old;
Old age hath yet his honor and his toil.
Death closes all; but something ere the end,
Some work of noble note, may yet be done,
Not unbecoming men that stove with Gods.
The lights begin to twinkle from the rocks;
The long day wanes; the slow moon climbs; the deep
Moans round with many voices. Come, my friends,
'Tis not too late to seek a newer world.

Push off, and sitting well in order smite
The sounding furrows; for my purpose holds
To sail beyond the sunset, and the baths
Of all the western stars, until I die.
It may be that the gulfs will wash us down;
It may be we shall touch the Happy Isles,
And see the great Achilles, whom we knew.
Though much is taken, much abides; and though
We are not now that strength which in old days
Moved earth and heaven, that which we are, we are:
One equal temper of heroic hearts,
Made weak by time and fate, but strong in will
To strive, to seek, to find, and not to yield.

—*Alfred, Lord Tennyson*

1. Describe the speaker in this poem.

2. Underline several lines that seem to capsulize the speaker's philosophy of life.

3. What kinds of people would be Ulysses' friends?

4. What does Tennyson seem to be saying about human aspirations to greatness?

Name_____

Date _____

Miniver Cheevy

Miniver Cheevy, child of scorn,
    Grew lean while he assailed the seasons;
He wept that he was ever born,
    And he had reasons.

Miniver loved the days of old
    When swords were bright and steeds were prancing;
The vision of a warrior bold
    Would set him dancing.

Miniver sighed for what he was not,
    And dreamed, and rested from his labors;
He dreamed of Thebes and Camelot,
    And Priam's neighbors.

Miniver mourned the ripe renown
    That made so many a name so fragrant;
He mourned Romance, now on the town,
    And Art, a vagrant.

Miniver loved the Medici,
    Albeit he had never seen one;
He would have sinned incessantly
    Could he have been one.

Miniver cursed the commonplace
    And eyed a khaki suit with loathing;
He missed the medieval grace
    Of iron clothing.

Miniver scorned the gold he sought,
    But sore annoyed was he without it;
Miniver thought, and thought, and thought,
    And thought about it.

Miniver Cheevy, born too late,
    Scratched his head and kept on thinking;
Miniver coughed, and called it fate,
    And kept on drinking.

—E. A. Robinson

1. Compare and contrast Miniver with Tennyson's Ulysses.

2. What does Robinson seem to be saying about human aspirations to greatness?

Ozymandias

I met a traveller from an antique land
Who said: "Two vast and trunkless legs of stone
Stand in the desert . . . Near them, on the sand,
Half sunk, a shattered visage lies, whose frown,
And wrinkled lip, and sneer of cold command,
Tell that its sculptor well those passions read
Which yet survive, stamped on these lifeless things;
The hand that mocked them, and the heart that fed:
And on the pedestal these words appear:
'My name is Ozymandias, king of kings:
Look on my works, ye Mighty, and despair!'
Nothing beside remains. Round the decay
Of that colossal wreck boundless and bare
The lone and level sands stretch far away."

—*Percy Bysshe Shelley*

1. What is the meaning of the inscription on the statue?

2. Identify the poem's central irony.

3. What does Shelley seem to imply about human aspirations to greatness?

Cemetery of Whales

A cemetery of whales:
    in a snowy graveyard
instead of crosses
    their own bones stand.
They couldn't be gnawed by teeth;
    teeth are too soft.
They couldn't be used for soup;
    pots are too shallow.
The straining wind bends them,
    but they keep their position,
rooted in ice,
    arching like black rainbows.
Thirsty for a snort,
    as Eskimo hunchback,
shaped like a question mark,
    huddles in them as in parentheses.
Who playfully clicked a camera?
    Restrain your photophilia.
Let's leave the whales in peace,
    if only after death.
They lived, these whales,
    without offense to people,
in infantile simplicity,
    reveling in their own fountains,
while the crimson ball of the sun
    danced in a torrent of rays . . .
Thar she blows!
    Come on, lads, let's get 'em.
Where can we hide?
    But you're broader than space!
The world doesn't hold enough water
    for you to dive under.
You think you're God?
    A risky bit of impudence.
One harpoon, smack in the flank,
    rewards enormity.
Enormity commands everyone
    to hunt for it.
Whoever is big is stupid.
    Who's smaller is wiser.
Sardines, like vermicelli,
    are an impossible target,
lost in the generic—
    but greatness is helpless.
On board, binoculars tremble
    as the crew takes aim;
streaming harpoon in his side,
    huge Tolstoy runs from the Kodak.
A baby whale, not full-fledged,
    though evaluated as a whale,
Esenin flutters and kicks,
    hoisted high on a harpoon shaft.
The title of whale is a bloody dignity.
    Greatness kills greatness.

Mayakovsky himself
    pounds in the lance.
The shallows are also a menace:
    dashed on the shoals by the chase,
Groky hawks and disgorges
    fragments of steel and hickory.
Without even moaning,
    gliding along the path of blood,
Pasternak with a snatch of lime
    sinks into Lethe.
Hemingway is silent;
    but from his grave a threatening shaft
shoots out of the grass,
    growing up from the coffin.
And hidden behind the mob,
    murder in his eye,
the Dallas whaler
    while a telescopic sight.
A big drive is on;
    we cherish their names posthumously.
Your law is more honest,
    cruel Alaska.
In the cemetery of whales
    by the hummocks of ice
there are no sanctimonious flowers:
    the Eskimos have tact.
Hey, Eskimo hunchback,
    white men have a funny custom:
After planting the harpoon,
    they weep over the corpse.
Murderers mourn like maidens,
    and tearfully suck tranquilizers,
and parade in crepe,
    and stand honor guard.
The professional hunters,
    who look out of place,
send wreaths to the whales
    from the State Bureau of Harpoonery.
But the flowers are twisted together
    with steel cable sand barbs.
Enough of such goodness!
    Let me live among Eskimos!
            —*Yevgeny Yevtushenko*
      translated by John Updike with Albert C. Todd

What does Yevtushenko imply about human greatness?

Lesson 26
Macbeth, Macduff, and Human Potential

Objective

- To enable students to recognize successful as well as unfulfilled human potentiality

Notes to the Teacher

This lesson assumes that Advanced Placement students are familiar with Shakespeare's *Macbeth* and have a thorough understanding of its events, particularly the rise and fall of Macbeth and Macduff's triumph over him.

Procedure

1. Using **Handout 48**, point out that throughout the play Macbeth's character declines, while the character of Macduff remains respected and admired.

2. Ask students to discuss Macbeth's and Macduff's potentiality for greatness and why one fails, while the other succeeds.

   Suggested Responses:

   Macbeth is a successful and admired general but becomes greedy for power.

   Macbeth places personal ambition before all else.

   Macduff has respect and justifies it through action by ridding Scotland of the hated Macbeth and restoring the rightful king to Scotland.

3. How does Shakespeare reveal Macbeth's rise and decline?

   He reveals it through adjectives used to describe him.

   How does Shakespeare reveal Macduff's staying power?

   His goodness is maintained through the play in other characters' references to him.

4. Ask students what characteristics humankind must possess for achievement of greatness in today's world. Record their ideas on the board.

5. Ask students to name well-known persons who represent achievement in human potential and those who have failed in achievement. Record responses on the board.

6. Ask students for suggestions of commonalities among their examples. Record responses on the board.

7. Ask students to formulate their own definitions of human greatness and its prerequisites in an informal essay.

Name_____

Date _____

Descriptive References to Macbeth and Macduff
from *Macbeth*

Macbeth	Macduff
. . . brave Macbeth—well he deserves that name . . . (1.2)	. . . good Macduff . . . (2.4)
. . . valiant cousin . . . (1.2)	. . . his wisdom . . . (3.2)
. . . worthiest cousin . . . (1.4)	He is noble, wise, judicious . . . (4.2)
. . . he is full so valiant . . . (1.6)	. . . the good Macduff . . . (5.2)
. . . We love him highly . . . (1.6)	. . . worthy Macduff . . . (5.6)
. . . his highness is not well . . . (3.4)	
. . . quite unmanned in folly? (3.4)	
. . . a wayward son/Spiteful and wrathful . . . (3.5)	
. . . bloody, luxurious, avaricious, false, deceitful,/Sudden, malicious, smacking of every sin . . . (4.3)	
. . . Devilish Macbeth . . . (4.3)	
. . . the tyrant . . . (4.3)	
. . . dwarfish thief . . . (5.3)	
. . . abhorred tyrant . . . (5.7)	
. . . coward . . . (5.8)	
. . . dead butcher . . . (5.8)	

Lesson 27
Human Potential: Questions and Answers

Objective

- To enable students to question human aspirations and to discover answer through literature

Notes to the Teacher

This lesson poses the questions that often arise in any thoughtful consideration of human potentiality and offers answers found in a variety of examples from literature. Students then have an opportunity to explore this method of synthesis through an essay assignment.

Procedure

1. Distribute **Handout 49** and review the questions.

2. Discuss examples from **Handout 50** to clarify the points. You may distribute this handout if you think that having students read these examples would be helpful.

3. Ask each student to select an interesting question from **Handout 49** and formulate an answer to that question in a well-organized essay. Advise students to document essays with support from literature.

Name_____

Date _____

Questions on Human Potential and Greatness

1. What universal qualities of individual greatness are most often explored by authors?

2. What reasons can you discover as to why some individuals reach greatness, others remain mediocre, and some fail?

3. Can you determine why certain individuals or characters who embody the qualities demanded of greatness sometimes fail to exhibit these characteristics?

4. Do most characters have the potential for greatness? Do they recognize this within themselves and strive to achieve greatness, or are they manipulated by the forces around them?

5. What situations call for greatness? Are there instances when a character withholds the potential for greatness?

6. Can the potential for greatness be learned, or is it inherent in most individuals or characters?

7. What limits does society place upon the degree of greatness that can be achieved?

8. How important is an individual's or character's background, education, health, intelligence, or determination in relation to the achievement of greatness?

9. Can an individual or character achieve greatness in private life, or must the greatness be recognized by others publicly?

10. Is greatness rewarded, or does it provide its own satisfaction?

Name_____

Date _____

Human Aspirations in Literature

Jude the Obscure
  Thomas Hardy

Jude's aspirations diminish from those of an idealistic young boy hoping for a future at Christminster. By the end of the novel, Christminster has become nothing more than a toy model for him.

All the King's Men
  Robert Penn Warren

Willie Stark's political achievement as state governor masks his interior fall to dishonesty and political graft. His assassination at the end of the novel is a form of punishment for his destruction of innocence.

A Raisin in the Sun
  Lorraine Hansberry

In this play, Mama and her family meet many obstacles in their attempt to achieve a better standard of living by moving to a white neighborhood. Walter feels his potential is thwarted by the black matriarchal system.

An Enemy of the People
  Henrik Ibsen

Dr. Stockmann is heady with his discovery of the bath's pollution. During the play, he becomes misguided in his unpopular achievement and overextends his authority. His aspirations misdirect him into sacrificial futility.

Cyrano de Bergerac
  Edmond Rostand

Cyrano wins the applause of the crowd as he somewhat arrogantly composes a poem as he wins a duel. His inner greatness leads him to sacrifice himself for the happiness of his beloved Roxanne.

Crime and Punishment
  Fyodor Dostoevsky

Raskolnikov believes that the extraordinary man is not bound by the laws of society. To prove to himself that he is such a man, he murders an old pawnbroker in order to distribute her wealth to the impoverished. Sonia, the daughter who becomes a prostitute to provide for her family, provides an alternative path to greatness through suffering.

Other examples from literature that deal with this theme include

Great Expectations
  Charles Dickens
The Grapes of Wrath
  John Steinbeck
Arms and the Man
Saint Joan
Man and Superman
  George Bernard Shaw
Exodus
  Leon Uris
Siddhartha
  Herman Hesse
The Emperor Jones
  Eugene O'Neill
Lord Jim
  Joseph Conrad
Return of the Native
  Thomas Hardy

Autobiography of Malcolm X
Heart of Darkness
  Joseph Conrad
The Old Man and the Sea
  Ernest Hemingway
A Man for All Seasons
  Robert Bolt
A Tale of Two Cities
  Charles Dickens
The Great Gatsby
  F. Scott Fitzgerald
Le Morte d'Arthur
  Sir Thomas Malory
The Natural
  Bernard Malamud
Zorba the Greek
  Nikos Kazantzakis

Epics: *The Epic of Gilgamesh*
  Beowulf
  The Illiad
  The Odyssey

Lesson 28
"I–Thou" Relationships

Objective

- To introduce students to Martin Buber's concept of "personal making present" and to apply it to "The Love Song of J. Alfred Prufrock" and to several short stories

Notes to the Teacher

Love is a concept that has been overused and underdefined in the English language. We "love" everything from a hot dog to a grandmother. The Greeks divided the concept of love into three types: *eros*, meaning sexual love; *philios*, meaning friendship love; and *agape*, meaning love of humanity. In a time when many marriage commitments are being broken by divorce, it seems appropriate to examine the nature and components of love that is committed to another person, whether in friendship, family, or marriage.

Martin Buber does not use the word *love* in his books that examine the "I–Thou" relationship. Yet, many of his readers see his understanding of the dimensions of personal commitment as the essentials of love. Writing in German, Buber calls his most famous concept "I–Thou" to emphasize both the one-to-one relationship that he defines and the intimacy of the relationship through the word *Thou*. In German, *Du (Thou)* is not an archaic term today. *Du* is used for the word *you*, however, only when a close personal relationship has been established between two people. The passage by Buber which is provided in this lesson is not from his most famous book, *I and Thou* (1923), but from a later work, *The Knowledge of Man* (1962), which is less poetic but more easily understood by students. Here he explicitly examines the nature of the "I–Thou" relationship of intimacy between two people who share each other's worlds and who truly meet in dialogue. Buber's term "personal making present" is, at least in its English translation, not easily understood. It means that when one person through dialogue is completely present to another person, the process of conferring acceptance and confirmation generates a more completely whole person; it is "personal making."

As is evident, the Buber passage is long and difficult. Its inclusion, however, seems justified because of its relevance to the concept of love and because it provides another passage of prose for skill development. Students should be reminded that although this translation refers only to the male gender, the female gender is understood.

You will want to obtain the short story "Rope" by Katherine Anne Porter. Students may read the story, or you may want to read it aloud to the class.

Procedure

1. Ask students to read **Handout 51**. Help them to understand Buber's concept through discussion of the following questions.

   a. Why do people usually make speeches instead of really speaking to each other?

      They are more interested in appearing good before the "fictitious court of appeal" than in hearing what the other person has to say.

   b. Which of the following would Buber allow in a dialogue-argument with a friend?

      1. You are stupid.

         Disallowed, does not confirm the person

      2. Your definition of "late" doesn't agree with mine!

         O.K.

      3. No one can ever count on you.

         Disallowed, does not confirm the person

      4. I'm sorry I ever started dating you; I should never have broken up with Ralph.

         Disallowed, does not confirm the person

      5. I become annoyed when you keep asking to copy my homework.

         O.K.

Help students to generalize that in dialogue, one argues about what a person thinks or does but not about who the person is. To criticize the act but not the person still affirms the partner, even though it attempts to change that person's behavior or convictions.

c. What difference does it make, according to Buber, that a human, alone of all things, has a spirit?

A human's spirit makes the human unique and thus a mystery that cannot be objectified because he or she is a dynamic center who is constantly changing and becoming more than he or she already is.

d. Explain how the three adjectives describing the look one modern human gives another are all belittling.

Analytical: *It pulls a person to pieces to focus on one part and forgets the whole.*

Reductive: *It reduces the human to a fixed stereotype that performs repetitive actions.*

Deriving: *It focuses on the general outline of what the person now is and forgets that the person is a growing, dynamic being.*

e. How does "imagining the real" give persons a new, more positive way of relating to each other?

When "imagining the real," one looks not only at what the person has become already but also at what the person hopes to become at his or her "dynamic center."

2. Alternative 1—Divide the class into listening triads. Designate each person in the triad A, B, and C. For the first round, A and B are to be in dialogue, with C the observer. A does the talking, and B responds in a "personal making present" way. After five minutes, C reports observations about whether or not B was affirming. Repeat two times until all three students have had a chance to talk. The subject of the dialogue should be a description of some love commitment the student knows well.

Alternative 2—Brainstorm with the class all of the characteristics of real dialogue and monologue/dialogue. List the characteristics in two columns on the board.

3. Distribute **Handout 52** to the class, and tell students that this is about one-fourth of a long poem by T. S. Eliot, who is famous for his descriptions of the aridity of relationships in the modern world. "The Love Song of J. Alfred Prufrock" is a dramatic monologue that characterizes the speaker, Prufrock, as a timid, limited man who is completely incapable of intimacy with anyone. The following approaches may help students apply Buber's concept, as it is not fulfilled, to Prufrock:

a. Prufrock, too, is afraid of Buber's "fictitious court of appeal whose life consists of nothing but listening to him." Discuss.

Evidence—Prufrock's "court of appeal" seems most concerned with his appearance: "They will say: 'How his hair is growing thin!'"

b. Prufrock has "known the eyes" that give him the analytical, reductive, and driving look. What metaphor does he use to describe this experience?

Metaphor of being pinned to the wall like an insect

How do "eyes . . . fix you in a formulated phrase"?

Prufrock never relates to a whole woman; here she is only "eyes," since this is where the threat comes from. These "eyes" also have a hurtful voice that puts him down with a "formulated phrase."

What is Prufrock's response to such a look-phrase?

He becomes disgusted with his entire life, which he wants to "spit out" and which he refers to in the metaphor "the butt-ends of my days and ways."

c. Prufrock, himself, is incapable of entering into dialogue with another whole person. Explain why.

Prufrock is too afraid that he is inadequate: "Do I dare?" He is unable to forget his own inadequacies in order to enter into a relationship which demands that his concentration be upon the whole person of another.

d. How does Prufrock see the women with whom he would like to fall in love?

In addition to calling them "eyes," Prufrock also calls them "arms."

Why is this all he sees of these women?

Their arms are what he wants—around him, rather than "[lying] along a table, or wrap[ping] about a shawl."

How would Buber think Prufrock should see these women?

As whole persons radiating from their dynamic centers, not as parts of the body he fears or needs (Prufrock both reduces women and objectifies them.)

4. Have students apply Buber's characteristics of an "I–Thou" relationship to the marriage in the short story "Rope" by Katherine Anne Porter. The following approaches may be useful:

a. Show how, in the first paragraph, each person gives his/her partner a "deriving look."

He calls her a "barn country woman," while she calls him a "rural character in a play."

Which response has more favorable connotations, and why might each respond as he/she does?

His response is more favorable, perhaps because he is more accepting of her or because he is happier to have moved into the country.

b. Buber advises us to be direct with each other, which implies that we should say what our real needs are. Which one of the couple is first to be direct?

He is, when he says, "Well, thunder, he had bought it because he wanted to, and that was all there was to it."

What indirect method of belittling does the wife use?

Irony—"Undoubtedly it would be useful . . . come in." "She was sure she begged his pardon . . . step on them in the dark." "It was a swell time . . . for him to get out from under." "Yes, yes she knew how it was with a man . . . naturally he couldn't hurt her feelings by refusing!" "She congratulated him: he must have a damned easy conscience." "Lord what an uproarious joke!"

c. Buber says the "reductive look" belittles by reducing the richness and uniqueness of the person to a type that simply performs repeated actions. Which partner uses this technique as a weapon most often?

The husband—". . . with her insane habit of changing things around and hiding them." "Did she realize she was making a complete fool of herself?" "The whole trouble with her was she needed something weaker than she was to heckle and tyrannize over . . . Maybe he'd get some rest." ". . . if she wasn't such a hopeless melancholiac she might see that this was only for a few days."

The wife, however, also uses this weapon—"If he told her they could manage somehow, she would certainly slap his face." "She was surprised he hadn't stayed in town as it was until she had come out and done the work and got things straightened out. It was his usual trick."

d. In what two instances does the wife probably misjudge her husband because she does not grasp what he has become?

First, she makes too much out of last summer's episode: "It was impossible to believe she was going to take it seriously." Second, she doesn't realize how much she hurt him when she told him the two weeks alone in the country were the happiest she had known for four years.

5. Assign a short story that dramatizes a successful love relationship where Buber's "I-Thou" relationship is demonstrated.

Suggestions:
J.D. Salinger's "For Esmè, with Love and Squalor" or Willa Cather's "Neighbor Rossicky" provide nice examples. Both Esmè and Rossicky, through their loving relationships, affect another person (Esmè affects the narrator; Rossicky affects Polly) so that person becomes more whole and/or accepting. These stories show how a dialogical relationship causes one partner to grow toward "wholeness, unity and uniqueness which are only partly developed, as is usually the case," as Buber says. The Salinger story, in addition, has a powerful negative example in "Clay" of a person who, like Prufrock, belittles the narrator. Wilbur Daniel Steele's "How Beautiful with Shoes," may also be used, although students may have difficulty seeing that Humble Jewett establishes a dialogical relationship with Amarantha which changes her in spite of her fear of him.

Other stories that provide negative examples
of people who do not or cannot establish an
"I–Thou" relationship are

"The Jockey"
    Carson McCullers
"I'm a Fool"
    Sherwood Anderson
"Hills Like White Elephants"
    Ernest Hemingway
"The Harness"
    John Steinbeck

"Eveline"
    James Joyce
"Theft"
    Katherine Anne Porter
"Unlighted Lamps"
    Sherwood Anderson
"The Eighty-Yard Run"
    Irwin Shaw
"The Sucker"
    Carson McCullers
"Virga Vay and Alan Cedar"
    Sinclair Lewis

Personal Making Present
Martin Buber

By far the greater part of what is today called conversation among men would
be more properly and precisely described as speechifying. In general, people do not
really speak to one another, but each, although turned to the other, really speaks
to a fictitious court of appeal whose life consists of nothing but listening to him.

He who really knows how far our generation has lost the way of true freedom,
of free giving between I and Thou, must himself, by virtue of the demand implicit
in every great knowledge of this kind, practice directness even if he were the only
man on earth who did it—and not depart from it until scoffers are struck with fear,
and hear in his voice the voice of their own suppressed longing.

The chief presupposition for the rise of genuine dialogue is that each should
regard his partner as the very one he is. I become aware of him, aware that he is
different, essentially different from myself, in the definite, unique way which is
peculiar to him, and I accept whom I thus see, so that in full earnestness I can direct
what I say to him as the person he is. Perhaps from time to time I must offer strict
opposition to his view about the subject of our conversation. But I accept this
person, the personal bearer of a conviction, in his definite being out of which his
conviction has grown—even though I must try to show, bit by bit, the wrongness of
this very conviction. I affirm the person I struggle with: I struggle with him as his
partner, I confirm him as creature and as creation, I confirm him who is opposed
to me as him who is over against me. It is true that it now depends on the other
whether genuine dialogue, mutuality in speech, arises between us. But if I thus give
to the other who confronts me his legitimate standing as a man with whom I am
ready to enter into dialogue, then I may trust him and suppose him to be also ready
to deal with me as his partner.

But what does it mean to be "aware" of a man in the exact sense in which I use
the word? To be aware of a thing or a being means, in quite general terms, to
experience it as a whole and yet at the same time without reduction or abstraction,
in all its concreteness. But a man, although he exists as a living being among living
beings and even as a thing among things, is nevertheless something categorically
different from all things and all beings. A man cannot really be grasped except on
the basis of the gift of the spirit which belongs to man alone among all things, the
spirit as sharing decisively in the personal life of the living man, that is, the spirit
which determines the person. To be aware of a man, therefore, means in particular
to perceive his wholeness as a person determined by the spirit; it means to perceive
the dynamic centre which stamps his every utterance, action, and attitude with the
recognizable sign of uniqueness. Such an awareness is impossible, however, if and
so long as the other is the separated object of my contemplation or even observation,
for this wholeness and its centre do not let themselves be known to contemplation
or observation. It is only possible when I step into an elemental relation with the
other, that is, when he becomes present to me. Hence I designate awareness in this
special sense as "personal making present."

The perception of one's fellow man as a whole, as a unity, and as unique—even
if his wholeness, unity and uniqueness are only partly developed, as is usually the
case—is opposed in our time by almost everything that is commonly understood as
specifically modern. In our time there predominates an analytical, reductive, and
deriving look between man and man. This look is a reductive one because it tries
to contract the manifold person, who is nourished by the microcosmic richness of
the possible, to some schematically surveyable and recurrent structures. And this

look is a deriving one because it supposes it can grasp what a man has become, or even is becoming, in genetic formulae, and it thinks that even the dynamic central principle of the individual in this becoming can be represented by a general concept. An effort is being made today radically to destroy the mystery between man and man. The personal life, the ever near mystery, once the source of the stillest enthusiasm, is levelled down.

If we want to do today's work and prepare tomorrow's with clear sight, then we must develop in ourselves and in the next generation a gift which lives in man's inwardness as a Cinderella one day to be a princess. Some call it intuition, but that is not a wholly unambiguous concept. I prefer the name "imagining the real," for in its essential being this gift is not a looking at the other, but a bold swinging—demanding the most intensive stirring of one's being—into the life of the other. This is the nature of all genuine imagining, only that here the realm of my action is not the all possible, but the particular real person who confronts me, whom I can attempt to make present to myself just in this way, and not otherwise, in his wholeness, unity, and uniqueness, and with his dynamic centre which realizes all these things ever anew.

Let it be said again that all this can only take place in a living partnership, that is, when I stand in a common situation with the other and expose myself vitally to his share in the situation as really his share. It is true that my basic attitude can remain unanswered, and the dialogue can die in seed. But if mutuality stirs, then the interhuman blossoms into genuine dialogue. [1]

[1]Martin Buber, "Personal Making Present," *The Knowledge of Man* (New York: Harper & Row, 1965), 78–81.

Name_____

Date _____

From "The Love Song of J. Alfred Prufrock"

In the room the women come and go
Talking of Michelangelo.

And indeed there will be time
To wonder, "Do I dare?" and, "Do I dare?"
Time to turn back and descend the stair,
With a bald spot in the middle of my hair—
They will say: "How his hair is growing thin!"
My morning coat, my collar mounting firmly to the chin,
My necktie rich and modest, but asserted by a simple pin—
They will say: "But how his arms and legs are thin!"
Do I dare
Disturb the universe?
In a minute there is time
For decisions and revisions which a minute will reverse.

For I have known them all already, known them all:—
Have known the evenings, mornings, afternoons,
I have measured out my life with coffee spoons;—
I know the voices dying with a dying fall
Beneath the music from a farther room
    So how should I presume?

And I have known the eyes already, known them all—
The eyes that fix you in a formulated phrase,
And when I am formulated, sprawling on a pin,
When I am pinned and wriggling on the wall,
Then how should I begin
To spit out all the butt-ends of my days and ways
    And how should I presume?

And I have known the arms already, known them all—
Arms that are braceleted and white and bare
But in the lamplight, downed with light brown hair!
Is it perfume from a dress
That makes me so digress?
Arms that lie along a table, or wrap about a shawl,
    And should I then presume?
    And how should I begin?

—*T. S. Eliot*

Lesson 29
Love Poems

Objective

- To have students extend their understanding of the thematic concern "love commitments" through an examination of four poems

Notes to the Teacher

Love poetry is a long tradition, reflecting the focus, since the Middle Ages, on love relationships as people's central concern and the basis of society. In this lesson, students consider four love poems and compare and contrast their treatments of love relationships.

Procedure

1. Have students read "Love Song: I and Thou" on **Handout 53**. Conduct a discussion using the following questions:

   a. The house described in the poem is metaphorical. What does it stand for? What does it look like? What is the speaker's attitude toward it?

   The speaker's life; crooked, askew; he accepts that this house, or life, unfinished as it is, is uniquely his

   b. At what point does this become an "I–Thou" love poem?

   The last two lines

   c. Describe the tone of the poem.

   Until the last few lines, the tone is ironic, exasperated; the last two lines are tender.

   d. The title of the poem alludes to Martin Buber's "I–Thou" relationship. How is this reflected in the poem itself?

   The speaker not only accepts the motley conditions of his own life but also accepts the necessity of sharing the realities of his life with another person.

   e. Do you feel that this poem is romantic?

   The poem is realistic, not romantic, about life and relationships.

2. Have students, working in groups of two or three, read the sonnets on **Handout 54** and answer the questions.

3. Review responses.

   Suggested Responses:

   1. *Sonnets; topic of romantic love; unending nature of love; love as the most important facet of a person's life*

   2. *Browning warmly addresses her beloved, while Shakespeare writes objectively about love. Thus, the tones of the poems contrast.*

   3. *While the sonnets are more romantic than Dugan's wry poem, they reflect some of the same viewpoints. Browning relates her love to everyday's most quiet need and recognizes that her life will involve both smiles and tears. Shakespeare recognizes that people do change and that love extends past beauty and youth to sickness and old age.*

4. Have students read and complete **Handout 55**.

5. Ask students to share responses.

Students may note the reverent tenderness of tone, the speaker's radical openness to the beloved, and his acceptance of mystery at the heart of the relationship.

Love Song: I and Thou

Nothing is plumb, level or square:
    the studs are bowed, the joists
are shaky by nature, no piece fits
    any other piece without a gap
or pinch, and bent nails
    dance all over the surfacing
like maggots. By Christ
    I am no carpenter. I built
the roof for myself, the walls
    for myself, the floors
for myself, and got
    hung up in it myself. I
danced with a purple thumb
    at this house-warming, drunk
with my prime whisky: rage.
    Oh I spat rage's nails
into the frame-up of my work:
    it held. It settled plumb,
level, solid, square and true
    for that one moment. Then
it screamed and went on through
    skewing as wrong the other way.
God damned it. This is hell,
    but I planned it, I sawed it,
I nailed it, and I
    will live in it until it kills me.
I can nail my left palm
    to the left-hand cross-piece but
I can't do everything myself.
    I need a hand to nail the right,
a help, a love, a you, a wife.

                —*Alan Dugan*

Two Famous Love Sonnets

XLII

How do I love thee? Let me count the ways.
I love thee to the depth and breadth and height
My soul can reach, when feeling out of sight
For the ends of Being and ideal Grace.
I love thee freely, as men strive for Right;
I love thee purely, as they turn from praise.
I love thee with the passion put to use
In my old griefs, and with my childhood's faith.

I love thee with a love I seemed to lose
With my lost saints,—I love thee with the breath,
Smiles, tears, of all my life!—and, if God choose,
I shall but love thee better after death.

—*Elizabeth Barrett Browning*

CXVI

Let me not to the marriage of true minds
Admit impediments. Love is not love
Which alters when it alteration finds,
Or bends with the remover to remove:
O, No! It is an ever-fixed mark
That looks on tempests and is never shaken'
It is the star to every wandering bark,
Whose worth's unknown, although his height be taken.
Love's not Time's fool, though rosy lips and cheeks
Within his bending sickle's compass come;
Love alters not with his brief hours and weeks,
But bears it out even to the edge of doom.
    If this be error and upon me proved,
    I never writ, nor no man ever loved.

—*William Shakespeare*

1. In what ways are these two love poems alike?

2. How do they differ?

3. Are they like or unlike Alan Dugan's poem?

Name_____

Date _____

LVII

somewhere i have never travelled, gladly beyond
any experience, your eyes have their silence;
in your most frail gesture are things which enclose me,
or which i cannot touch because they are near

your slightest look easily will unclose me
though i have closed myself as fingers,
you open always petal by petal myself as spring opens
(touching skillfully, mysteriously) her first rose

or if your wish be to close me, i and
my life will shut very beautifully, suddenly,
as when the heart of this flower imagines
the snow carefully everywhere descending;

nothing which we are to perceive in this world equals
the power of your intense fragility: whose texture
compels me with the colour of its countries,
rendering death and forever with each breathing

(i do not know what it is about you that closes
and opens; only something in me understands
the voice of your eyes is deeper than all roses)
nobody, not even the rain, has such small hands

—*e. e. cummings*

What does this poem say about "I–Thou" relationships?

Lesson 30
Examining Love Commitments

Objective

- To strengthen students' awareness of the commitments that occur in loving relationships found in literature

Notes to the Teacher

This lesson culminates this section with a series of questions regarding love commitments and accompanying examples from literature. Students examine the questions, consider the literary examples, and draw conclusions or formulate opinions of their own.

Procedure

1. Review questions on **Handout 56**.

2. Ask students to consider the examples from literature on **Handout 57** and discuss the validity of the relationships contained therein. Do any fit Buber's "I–Thou" model ?

3. Ask students to discuss love relationships as depicted in current films or in television series. Suggest that these relationships reflect modern society's general failure to live by the "I–Thou" mode.

4. Assign students in pairs to write creative short pieces in which they place characters of their own invention in an "I–Thou" relationship.

5. Distribute **Handout 58**. After enough reading time, ask students to explore situations where potentially fatal decisions about loved ones are considered. This activity may end with class discussion or a writing assignment.

Questions on Love Commitments

1. When can you know that a character in literature truly loves another?

2. How do authors treat the theme of love in all its varieties? Which type of love seems more evident in your readings? *Eros? Philia? Agape?*

3. Which works of literature indicate that loving another is sometimes painful, sometimes demanding, sometimes futile?

4. When is love more a sense of duty than a real desire to help another person become all that person can be?

5. Why do many people have trouble expressing honest emotions of love?

6. Why does there seem to be more significant literature dealing with the darker aspects of love than the "happily ever after" types?

7. What are some of the dictates our society imposes on love relationships? What are some commercial aspects of love relationships?

8. Must you love yourself before you can love another person?

9. Do you agree with Tennyson's observation from "In Memoriam" that "It is better to have loved and lost/ Than never to have loved at all?"

10. A lasting love commitment is a major goal and need in life. What are some of the impediments that make this goal and need difficult to obtain?"

Name_____

Date _____

Love Commitments in Literature

Anna Karenina
  Leo Tolstoy

Anna Karenina presents several interesting marriage and/or love relationships. Kitty and Levin are examples of a genuine "I–Thou" love commitment. Oblonsky and Dolly, Anna and Karenina, and Anna and Vronsky exemplify a variety of relational weaknesses.

Hedda Gabler
  Henrik Ibsen

Hedda's marriage to George Tesman is a travesty; he does not really know her, and she scorns him. Her relationship with Eilert Lovborg is exploitative. Thea's attitude, first toward Lovborg, latter toward Tesman, is much closer to Buber's "I–Thou" ideal.

Sons and Lovers
  D. H. Lawrence

With sensitive Miriam, Paul experiences a partial "I–Thou" relationship in a totally spiritual communion. On the other hand, although his relationship with Clara is passionate and sexually fulfilling, Paul cannot share with her the things that are important to him.

Madame Bovary
  Gustav Flaubert

To escape the drudgery of her family home, Emma marries a cloddish doctor. Dissatisfied, she romanticizes and turns to Rodolphe, who trifles with her affections. Finally, she has a third unsatisfactory affair with Leon. Emma tries frantically to find her ideal of love, but none of her three relationships come close to Buber's ideal.

The following novels are among the many other literary works that deal with this theme.

The French Lieutenant's Woman
  John Fowles

A Passage to India
  E. M. Forster

Dr. Zhivago
  Boris Pasternak

Far from the Madding Crowd
  Thomas Hardy

East of Eden
  John Steinbeck

Pygmalion
  George Bernard Shaw

Kristin Lavrensdatter
  Sigrid Undset

Twelfth Night
  William Shakespeare

The Taming of the Shrew
  William Shakespeare

Investigation of the Love Commitment in
Of Mice and Men

John Steinbeck took the title for this novel from lines of a poem entitled "To a Mouse" by Robert Burns: "The best laid schemes o' mice and men/ Gang aft agley" (often go astray). In this novel, George and Lennie's plans go astray. In Steinbeck's novel, George kills Lennie, whom he loves very much. Readers can assume he does this because he wishes to protect Lennie from Curly's lynch mob or from conviction and imprisonment over the accidental death of Curly's wife. However, we all know that murder is the antithesis of love.

Oscar Wilde wrote in his "Ballad of Reading Gaol" that "Each man kills the thing he loves/ By each let this be heard . . . The coward does it with a kiss/ The brave man with a sword."

Question
Can you reconcile these views found in Oscar Wilde's poetry and enacted in Steinbeck's novel with what you know of love?

Lesson 31
War and Literature

Objectives

- To demonstrate that the horror of war is often subject matter in literature
- To enable students to react and respond to examples of such literature

Notes to the Teacher

The idea that "war is hell" is not a new one. Throughout history, no matter how glorious the cause, war has demanded devastating costs in human lives and property for all parties involved.

These costs, this destruction, and this waste have been favored topics of writers who hope to expose the piteous folly of war. As far back as Homer's *Iliad*, the pain of war has been forever etched into the anthologies of human endeavor. Perhaps no other subject has such broad application in a study of the human condition, as few of the world's civilizations have remained unscarred by war's destructive forces.

The lesson that follows uses poetry, a short story, and novels to illustrate the attitude literature conveys about war.

You will want to obtain the short story "The Sniper" by Liam O'Flaherty and make it available to your students. Students may read the story in preparation of the lesson, or you may want them to read it in class as is suggested. "The Sniper" can be found in The Center for Learning's *The Short Story*.

Procedure

1. Distribute copies of **Handout 59**. Ask students to summarize Hardy's poetic monologue about World War I.

   Suggested Response:

   In a battle situation we kill people we don't know, who, under peaceful conditions, we might find are very much like ourselves.

2. Discuss "Dulce et Decorum Est" with the class. Point out that the last two lines of Owen's poem translate as "It is sweet and proper to die for one's country." This thought is attributed to Horace. Ask pairs of students to debate why Owens calls this thought an "old lie," in the face of patriotic duty in World War I.

3. Discuss "Innocence" with the class. Ask students to cite lines which indicate that we can become so indoctrinated and desensitized that war's horrors go unnoticed.

   Suggested Response:

   The young soldier retains his particular innocence; he views another man's horrifying death with detachment and feels nothing more than awareness of the cold weather.

4. Read aloud Liam O'Flaherty's short story, "The Sniper," or have students read it silently. After students have heard or read the story, discuss it in relation to the concept of war.

5. Lead students into a discussion of other ironic aspects of war.

   Suggested Responses:

   - *Agent Orange, used as a defoliate during the Viet Nam conflict, now threatens the lives of American soldiers who assisted in its application.*
   - *The atomic bombs that were dropped on Hiroshima and Nagasaki, Japan, and brought an end to World War II, have since been further developed by other nations and pose a definite threat to world peace.*
   - *The construction of missile sites greatly strengthens a location's economy, but that location becomes a likely target for foreign missiles.*

6. Distribute **Handout 60,** and ask students to complete the handout following the models suggested. After completion, ask for an oral sharing of ideas.

7. Ask students to write well-organized essays in which they summarize the common attitudes most authors generate toward war, and indicate how these attitudes may conflict with a sense of patriotism.

Name_____

Date _____

Poems about War

The Man He Killed

Had he and I but met
By some old ancient inn,
We should have sat us down to wet
Right many a nipperkin!

But ranged as infantry,
And staring face to face,
I shot at him as he at me,
And killed him in his place.

I shot him dead because—
Because he was my foe,
Just so: my foe of course he was;
That's clear enough; although

He thought he'd 'list, perhaps,
Offhand like,—just as I—
Was out of work—had sold his traps—
No other reason why.

Yes; quaint and curious war is!
You shoot a fellow down
You'd treat if met where any bar is,
Or help to half-a-crown.

—*Thomas Hardy*

Name_____

Date _____

Dulce et Decorum Est

Bent double, like old beggars under sacks,
Knock-kneed, coughing like hags, we cursed through sludge,
Till on the haunting flares we turned our backs,
And toward our distant rest began to trudge.
Men marched asleep. Many had lost their boots,
But limped on, blood-shod. All went lame, all blind;
Drunk with fatigue; deaf even to the hoots
Of gas shells dropping softly behind.
Gas! Gas! Quick, boys!—An ecstasy of fumbling,
Fitting the clumsy helmets just in time,
And flound'ring like a man in fire or lime.
Dim through the misty panes and thick green light,
As under a green sea, I saw him drowning.
In all my dreams before my helpless sight
He plunges at me, guttering, choking, drowning.
If in some smothering dreams, you too could pace
Behind the wagon that we flung him in,
And watch the white eyes wilting in his face,
His hanging face, like a devil's sick on sin,
If you could hear, at every jolt, the blood
Come gargling from the froth-corrupted lungs
Bitten as the cud
Of vile, incurable sores on innocent tongues,—
My friend, you would not tell with such high zest
To children ardent for some desperate glory,
The old lie: *Dulce et decorum est*
Pro patria mori.

—*Wilfred Owen*

Innocence

He ran the course and as he ran he grew,
And smelt his fragrance in the field. Already,
Running he knew the most he ever knew,
The egotism of a healthy body.
Ran into manhood, ignorant of the past:
Culture of guilt and guilt's vague heritage,
Self-pity and the soul; what he possessed
Was rich, potential, like the bud's tipped rage.
The Corps developed, it was plain to see,
Courage, endurance, loyalty and skill
To a morale firm as morality,
Hardening him to an instrument, until
The finitude of virtues that were there
Bodied within the swarthy uniform
A compact innocence, child-like and clear,
No doubt could penetrate, no act could harm.
When he stood near the Russian partisan
Being burned alive, he therefore could behold
The ribs wear gently through the darkening skin
And sicken only at the Northern cold,
Could watch the fat burn with a violet flame
And feel disgusted only at the smell,
And judge that all pain finishes the same
As melting quietly by his boots it fell.

—*Thom Gunn*

Name_____

Date _____

Novels at War with War

Write your own summaries of as many novels as you are able. Follow the examples given.

Title—*The Red Badge of Courage*   Author—Stephen Crane

Summary—A young man's courage is tested and defined as he witnesses and actively participates in injury and death on the battlefields of the Civil War.

Title—*Slaughterhouse Five*   Author—Kurt Vonnegut

Summary—As a prisoner of war in Dresden, Germany, during World War II, Billy Pilgrim witnesses the destruction of that defenseless city, known for hundreds of years for its delicate art work in porcelain.

Suggested titles and authors

All Quiet on the Western Front
    Erich Remarque

Endgame
    Samuel Beckett

The Sun Also Rises
    Ernest Hemingway

Friendly Persuasion
    Jessamyn West

War and Peace
    Leo Tolstoy

The Deer Hunter
    E. M. Corder

Lesson 32
Oppression of Minorities

Objective

- To enable students to see minority oppression and the struggle for rights as recurrent thematic concerns

Notes to the Teacher

A major recurring concern in literature is the plight of the poor and oppressed. The tendency of the powerful to exploit minority groups seems to be universal, spanning all ages and countries. Sometimes writers concern themselves directly and primarily with this issue. At other times, the subject is approached more obliquely or as a subordinate concern.

In this lesson, students use a variety of short selections as a basis for discussing minority oppression as a thematic concern. Students then relate the theme to novels and plays.

Procedure

1. Have students read **Handout 61**.

2. Conduct a discussion of the excerpts. Use the following questions as a way to begin discussion.

   a. These excerpts reflect the cultures of vastly different times and places. What do they have in common?

   Concern for people who are oppressed by the social system

   b. What kinds of people tend to be oppressed?

   Minorities, the poor, the different, the uneducated, the transient

   c. What are some examples of groups that have been or are still being oppressed?

   Indians, Hispanics, Jews, African Americans, Irish, Polish, Catholics, among many others

   d. Why does the system tend to oppress groups?

   Fear, greed, cruelty, pride

   e. According to the Book of Exodus, the Israelites were led out of Egypt by Moses, who has emerged as an archetypical hero and savior. Who are some other Moses figures who have helped to free oppressed people?

   Harriet Tubman; Martin Luther King, Jr.; Cesar Chavez

3. Point out that many works of literature deal either directly or indirectly with this kind of oppression.

4. Have students read and complete **Handout 62**.

5. Review the handout.

   Suggested Responses:

   "Incident"

   1. *This relatively small event had a big effect on the narrator. It also reflects a big social problem.*

   2. *The lines are wistful and make the reader empathize with the speaker.*

   3. *It shows how children absorb and suffer from the ills of their society.*

   "I, Too"

   1. *Both poems present the scorned African-American child.*

   2. *The second poem incorporates hope for a better future.*

   3. *The first poem does not deal with solutions, although it may imply that changes in the young could be the key to a better future. The second poem includes two solutions: increasing strength among African Americans and a change of heart among whites.*

6. Ask students to suggest the titles of novels and plays that deal with the thematic concern, the plight of the oppressed.

Examples:

The Diary of Anne Frank, Native Son, The Fixer, The Adventures of Huckleberry Finn, To Kill a Mockingbird, Light in August, The Jungle

7. Ask students to make a general statement about the position great literary works tend to take on minority oppression.

The works tend to condemn the oppression and emphasizieits unfairness and ultimate futility.

Optional Activity

Write a critical essay showing how one oppressed minority is presented in three or more literary works.

Oppression of Minorities: A Theme in Literature

In Leo Tolstoy's *Anna Karenina*, Nicolay Levin says the following to his brother, Konstantin:

> You know that capital oppresses the laborer. The laborers with us, the peasants, bear all the burden of labor, and are so placed that however much they work they can't escape from their position of beasts of burden. All the profits of labor, on which they might improve their position, and gain leisure for themselves, and after that education, all the surplus values are taken from them by the capitalists. And society's so constituted that the harder they work, the greater the profit of the merchants and landowners, while they stay beasts of burden to the end. And that state of things must be changed.

These words express a subordinate concern in this novel: society's tendency to exploit the powerless. The peasants in tsarist Russia were virtually enslaved in agricultural work.

John Steinbeck's *The Grapes of Wrath* is concerned primarily with the plight of the Okies, dispossessed farmers forced into becoming migrant workers. Steinbeck describes the deprivation and the desperation of the migrants, as well as the hard system that exploits them.

> They were hungry and they were fierce. And they had hoped to find a home, and they found only hatred. Okies—the owners hated them because the owners knew they were soft and the Okies strong, that they were fed and the Okies hungry; and perhaps the owners had heard from their grandfathers how easy it is to steal land from a soft man if you are fierce and hungry and armed. The owners hated them. They had nothing. And the laboring people hated Okies because a hungry man must work, and if he must work, if he has to work, the wage payer automatically gives him less for his work; and then no one can get more.

> And the dispossessed, the migrants, flowed into California, two hundred and fifty thousand, and three hundred thousand. Behind them new tractors were going on the land and the tenants were being forced off. And new waves were on the way, new waves of the dispossessed and the homeless, hardened, intent, and dangerous.

> And while the Californians wanted many things; accumulation, social success, amusement, luxury, and a curious banking security, the new barbarians wanted only two things—land and food; and to them the two were one.

The biblical book of Exodus describes the Israelites' enslavement by the Egyptians:

> Then there came to power in Egypt a new king who knew nothing of Joseph. "Look," he said to his subjects, "these people, the sons of Israel, have become so numerous and strong that they are a threat to us. We must be prudent and take steps against their increasing any further, or if war should break out, they might add to the number of our enemies. They might take arms against us and so escape out of the country." Accordingly they put slave drivers over the Israelites to wear them down under heavy loads. In this way they built the store cities of Pithon and Rameses for Pharaoh. But the more they were crushed, the more they increased and spread, and men came to dread the sons of Israel. The Egyptians forced the sons of Israel into slavery, and made their lives unbearable with hard labor, work with clay and brick, all kinds of work in the fields: they forced on them every kind of labor . . .

Pharaoh gave this command to the people's slave drivers and to the overseers. "Up to the present, you have provided these people with straw for brickmaking. Do so no longer; let them go and gather straw for themselves. All the same you are to get from them the same number of bricks as before, not reducing it at all. They are lazy, and that is why their cry is, 'Let us go and offer sacrifice to our God.' Make these men work harder than ever, so that they do not have time to stop and listen to glib speeches."

The people's slave drivers went out with the overseers to speak to the people. "Pharaoh has given orders," they said: "I will not provide you with straw. Go out and collect straw for yourselves wherever you can find it. But your output is not to be any less." So the people scattered all over the land of Egypt to gather stubble for making chopped straw. The slave drivers harassed them. "Every day you must complete your daily quota," they said, "just as you did when straw was provided for you." And the foremen who had been appointed for the sons of Israel by Pharaoh's slave drivers were flogged, and they were asked, "Why have you not produced your full amount of bricks as before, either yesterday or today?"

—Exodus 1:8–14; 5:6–14

Protest Poems

Incident

Once riding in old Baltimore
    Heart-filled, head-filled with glee,
I saw a Baltimorean
    Keep looking straight at me.

Now I was eight and very small,
    And he was no whit bigger,
And so I smiled, but he poked out
    His tongue, and called me, "Nigger."

I saw the whole of Baltimore
    From May until December;
Of all the things that happened there
    That's all that I remember.

                    —Countee Cullen

1. Why is this poem entitled "Incident"?

2. How do the last two lines affect you?

3. How does this poem deal with the thematic concern, oppression of minorities?

I, Too

I, too, sing America.
I am the darker brother.
They send me to eat in the kitchen
When company comes,
But I laugh,
And eat well,
And grow strong.
Tomorrow,
I'll be at the table
When company comes.
Nobody'll dare
Say to me,
"Eat in the kitchen,"
Then.
Besides,
They'll see how beautiful I am
And be ashamed—
I, too, am America.

—*Langston Hughes*

1. How is this poem similar to "Incident"?

2. How do the two poems differ?

3. Do the poems suggest any solutions?

Lesson 33
Reality or Illusion:
It's a Matter of Perception

Objectives

- To sharpen students' awareness of their encounters with illusion
- To recognize that the comparison of reality and illusion is not a comparison of good and evil

Notes to the Teacher

This lesson provides an opportunity for students to investigate the role illusion plays in different areas of their lives. This is a time for heightened awareness, not shocking discovery. Approach this topic of reality and illusion, which is so dominant in literature, as an enjoyable experience. Provide a nonthreatening classroom atmosphere, and avoid judgments.

Procedure

1. Circulate a number of dictionaries, and ask students to check the definitions of *reality* and *illusion*. Discuss common words used in the definitions, and write a list of the words on the board.

2. Ask students to write definitions of *reality* and *illusion* that reflect their own understanding of the terms. Share aloud.

3. Have students complete **Handout 63**. Encourage students' efforts to pantomime, and treat students' examples of illusions carefully.

Suggested Responses:

1. *Houdini, Blackstone, David Copperfield, Mr. Mephisto*

3. *Better looks and smell, more appeal, camouflaging of defects, youthful appearance, all of which can aid the user's sense of security; yes*

4. *The good life, social ease, self-actualization, women's liberation, virility, machoism, good friends, good times; tobacco, beer, liquor; misuse, over-consumption, can cause lung cancer or alcoholism*

5. *Candy bars, some cosmetic items; to see more of the product*

4. Ask students to privately consider the ways in which love has elements of both illusion and reality. Using their own definitions of *illusion* and *reality* from procedure 2, ask students to match these with various love relationships. Ask students to write a summary of their findings. You may ask for a class sharing of ideas, depending upon the class attitude, or they may keep these writings private.

5. Ask students to keep a record of various examples of reality and illusion as they encounter them for three days. Conduct a class sharing at the end of that time.

Commonly Encountered Illusions

1. All magical tricks are based on the idea of illusion. A first law among magicians is not to reveal the method used in the magical performance, so as not to destroy the illusion. We are entertained when the magician's assistant appears to be sawed into sections, birds fly out of top hats, or large items disappear.

   Name as many magicians as you can, and describe their mystifying tricks you have seen on stage or television.

2. Pantomime is a universal method of entertainment that requires much practice in creating an illusion of a plausible movement. A mime's performance is judged by how well he or she soundlessly creates a situation that evokes an emotional response from the audience. The Frenchman Marcel Marceau and the American team of Shields and Yarnell are very accomplished pantomime artists.

   Think for a few moments, and then pantomime a specific activity for the rest of your class. You may select an ordinary human activity, such as laughter, play, dance, or eating. Try to be true-to-life, but remember, no sound!

3. The cosmetic industry is one of America's largest money-makers. The use of cosmetics is widely accepted. What do cosmetics promise the user? Do the cosmetics deliberately create illusions?

4. What illusions do tobacco and liquor corporations use to sell their products? What are some specific products that create those illusions? What are the realities?

5. Packaging is very carefully considered by manufacturers before their products go out for sale. Sometimes after we unwrap all the packaging, we find the quantity of the product is not as great as it appeared to be—another illusion. What are some products that prove this to be true? What is the purpose of this use of illusion?

6. Often the way a person acts is an attempt to create a personality that conceals an undesired reality. For example, a professional football player may present an illusion of bravery or courage, when, in reality, he may be very frightened of injury during the game. A very outgoing individual who is always socially prominent may be concealing a shy personality. Often, the class clown or the class hoodlum may be avoiding the reality of insecurity by presenting the illusion of a person very much in control. What other examples of the use of illusion can you think of? Keep in mind that people usually develop illusions as needed.

7. Our point of view influences our perception of society. A simple visual example is evident in yearbooks, when photographers use a low-angle shot to make basketball players appear to be even taller.

   However, a more complicated discussion of point of view will center on personal bias, prejudices, socioeconomic status, level of self-respect, and other aspects of our character that influence our perceptions. For example, a plate of ham and beans may be viewed quite differently by a gourmet, a starving person, or a vegetarian.

   Give some examples to explain this element of illusion.

8. Illusion also occurs in the factual world of science. For example, a study in physics reveals the illusionary properties of light when viewed through a prism. Or perhaps you have perceived what appears to be water across the road while driving on a hot day. Can you think of other examples of illusions of this type?

Lesson 34
Reality and Illusion as Literary Concerns

Objective

- To have students examine the relationship between reality and illusion as a significant literary concern

Notes to the Teacher

Having considered reality and illusion as facets of everyday life, students are prepared to examine them as literary concerns. Poets, novelists, and playwrights often deal with various facets of these polarities: human tendencies to confuse the two; deliberate illusions that lead to terrible realities; deliberate illusions that reveal truth; choosing between reality and illusion. In this lesson, students probe four short selections for insights into the paradoxes of reality and illusion. If you have access to a trick mirror similar to those in fun houses and amusement parks, you may consider mounting it near the entrance to the classroom.

Procedure

1. Have students read **Handout 64**.

2. Use these questions to conduct a discussion of the poem:

   a. What situation does the poem present?

   The speaker is posing in front of a trick mirror like those used in fun houses and amusement parks.

   b. Why do people enjoy using these trick mirrors?

   For the fun of it! The images' distortions are amusing.

   c. Why, then, don't most people equip their homes with these amusing mirrors?

   Although they are amusing, there is something horrible and hallucinatory about the images.

   d. How does the speaker here ultimately react to the mirror?

   The speaker rejects its "tricks" in favor of the practicality of the usual flat mirror.

   e. What is the significance of the last two lines?

   The speaker recognizes reality, not "wonderland," as the setting for real living. At the same time, "bubble of the world" seems to imply that reality itself is permeated with illusions.

3. Have students read and complete **Handout 65**.

4. Review responses.

Suggested Responses:

"Richard Cory"

1. *The people thought that Richard Cory had the perfect life with everything anyone could want: dignity, good looks, humanity, glamour, money, grace, and power.*

2. *Cory seemed to have deliberately created this impression.*

3. *His suicide makes it clear that his life, far from being perfect, must have been filled with pain and frustration.*

4. *People often want to look good, to give an impression that they are completely happy and successful.*

5. *Sometimes reality and illusion are radically different. Illusions cannot ultimately substitute for reality. The idea that happiness can be bought is an illusion.*

"Constantly Risking Absurdity"

1. *The poet is compared to a trapeze artist.*

2. *The illusion here is deliberately created in order to reach truth and beauty.*

3. In "Richard Cory," illusion is used to mask reality. The poem presents an ironic contrast between appearance and reality. In "Constantly Risking Absurdity," the relationship between illusion and reality is paradoxical: the poet transcends reality in order to reach truth and beauty.

5. Point out that everyone's understanding of self, others, and life includes elements of both reality and illusion. There are times, though, when an experience of disillusionment is essential. Sometimes the inability to distinguish illusion from reality can lead to very serious consequences. Discuss this idea. Focus on the concept that this situation recurs in both life and serious literature.

6. Have students read and complete **Handout 66**.

7. Ask volunteers to share responses.

Suggested Responses:

1. *Realities—Kitty's past relationship with Levin; her feelings about both men; a "misty" future*

   Illusion—the idea of living happily ever after

2. *Some students may note that Kitty's understanding of love is illusory, so she is not yet ready for a love commitment.*

   If students have read Anna Karenina, *you may want to extend the discussion to a consideration of how Kitty confuses the glamour of infatuation with the reality of genuine love.*

Framed by the Wavy Mirror

I am all head like a trout observed
straight-on. This fish-face has mooned
at me before from polished doorknobs;
Cyclops—single-eyed but double-nosed.
"Advance." My head soars gothically
until it mushrooms where the glass bends:
atomic Hazo. "Retreat." Cyclops again.
"Face right." My head shrinks to a bean.
on trousered stilts. "Face about."
I sprout a ball-belly, rocking
like a balloon that will always land
on duck-feet. To hell with tricks.
Give me a flat glass that lets me count
my whiskers, preen and pat myself
with talc and stare at eyeballs staring
back. I spot it like an old assurer
on a globe that bowls a thousand worlds
of bubble gum. "Grin back, old twin."
What lives in wonderland dies fast.
The bubble of the world is waiting.

—*Samuel Hazo*

Name_____

Date _____

Richard Cory

Whenever Richard Cory went down town,
We people on the pavement looked at him:
He was a gentleman from sole to crown,
Clean favored, and imperially slim.
And he was always quietly arrayed,
And he was always human when he talked;
But still he fluttered pulses when he said,
"Good-morning," and he glittered when he walked.
And he was rich—yes, richer than a king—
And admirably schooled in every grace:
In fine, we thought that he was everything
To make us wish that we were in his place.
So on we worked, and waited for the light,
And went without the meat, and cursed the bread;
And Richard Cory, one calm summer night,
Went home and put a bullet through his head.

—Edwin Arlington Robinson

1. What impressions did the townspeople have about Richard Cory?

2. Why did they have those impressions?

3. How do we know that their view of Richard Cory was illusion, not reality?

4. What reasons might Cory have had for creating illusions about himself?

5. What does this poem say about reality and illusion?

6. Why is this poem so powerful?

Name_____

Date _____

Constantly Risking Absurdity

          Constantly risking absurdity
      and death
            whenever he performs
      above the heads
      of his audience   5
            the poet like an acrobat
      climbs on rime
      to a high wire of his own making
      and balancing on eyebeams
      above a sea of faces   10
                paces his way
      to the other side of day
            performing entrechats
      and all without mistaking
      anything   15
      for what it may not be
            For he's the super realist
      who must perforce perceive
                taut truth
      before the taking of each stance or step 20
            in his supposed advance
      toward that still higher perch
      where Beauty stands and waits
      with gravity
      to start her death-defying leap   25
      And he
      a little charleychaplin man
      who may or may not catch
      her fair eternal form
      spreadeagle in the empty air   30
      of existence

                        —*Lawrence Ferlinghetti*

1. What is the fundamental comparison in this poem?

2. Examine lines 14–25. What relationship do they express between reality and illusion?

3. How does this view of reality and illusion differ from the view in "Richard Cory?"

Name_____

Date _____

Reality and Illusion in Tolstoy

Early in Leo Tolstoy's *Anna Karenina*, Kitty, a young girl, finds herself choosing between two young men. Tolstoy describes her thoughts:

> She felt that this evening, when they would both meet for the first time, would be a turning-point in her life. And she was continually picturing them to herself, at one moment each separately, and then both together. When she mused on the past, she dwelt with pleasure, with tenderness, on the memories of her relations with Levin. The memories of childhood and of Levin's friendship with her dead brother gave a special poetic charm to her relations with him. His love for her, of which she felt certain, was flattering and delightful to her; and it was pleasant for her to think of Levin. In her memories of Vronsky there always entered a certain element of awkwardness, though he was in the highest degree well-bred and at ease, as though there were some false note—not in Vronsky, he was very simple and nice, but in herself, while with Levin she felt perfectly simple and clear. But, on the other hand, directly she thought of the future with Vronsky, there arose before her a perspective of brilliant happiness; with Levin the future seemed misty.

1. What elements of reality and illusion can you discern in this passage?

2. Which man do you think Kitty should choose? Or is she ready for a choice at all?

Lesson 35
Reality and Illusion in Three Major Literary Works

Objective

- To enable students to recognize that the concepts of reality and illusion provide the basis for some great literary works

Notes to the Teacher

This lesson assumes that students are familiar with *Oedipus the King*, *The Great Gatsby*, and *The Glass Menagerie*. This lesson does not attempt to teach these literary works but to explore further the author's uses of reality and illusion.

Procedure

1. Review with students their prior reading of *Oedipus the King* by Sophocles. A filmstrip may be used as a tool of review but not as a substitute for reading the play.

2. Have students complete **Handout 67** either individually or in small groups. Ask volunteers to share responses.

   Suggested Responses:

   1. *No. Believing in his perception of reality has brought him happiness.*

   2. *Oedipus wants to know what can be done to destroy the pestilence but has no indication that he is to blame. Oedipus reacts only as a good, caring king to save the people of Thebes. He has no idea that the pestilence is another phase of the original curse.*

   3. *Sophocles uses the blindness of Tiresias and Oedipus to indicate that the mere visual element does not always equip us to see what is reality and what is illusion. What we are able to perceive may be deceptive, so we cannot depend on visual interpretation but must go beyond that.*

3. Review with students their prior reading of *The Great Gatsby* by F. Scott Fitzgerald. A filmstrip may be helpful but will not substitute for reading the novel.

4. Ask students to complete **Handout 68** individually or in small groups. Ask students to share responses.

   Suggested Responses:

   1. *Fitzgerald illustrates that when our illusions are so intense that they become the sole reason for being, we can deny reality and even be willing to sacrifice our own beings for the perpetuation of illusion.*

   2. *Fitzgerald situated the sign with the huge eyes and corrective lenses (hence perfect vision) so that the characters in the novel must pass before it and even staged Myrtle's homicide before the stare of the sign. This focuses juxtaposition of the god-figure, an illusion, with the actual events, the reality.*

   3. *Because an illusion can be given credibility and life by the one who perceives it as such, we can create belief where we want it to be, even in a void.*

   4. *Through this encounter, we learn a lot about Gatsby and the illusions he creates. One thing that we learn, for example, is that the beautiful books with which he has filled his library are not cut. Thus, although he creates the illusion that he is well-read, none of the books have been read. The man with the "owl-eyed spectacles" sees beyond created illusions. He sees reality. He sees illusion that has been created, and he realizes it as such.*

5. Review with students their prior reading of *The Glass Menagerie* by Tennessee Williams. A filmstrip may be helpful but will not substitute for reading the play.

189

6. Ask students to complete **Handout 69** individually or in small groups. Ask volunteers to share responses.

Suggested Responses:

1. *The curtain softens the harshness of reality, while Tom maintains that the reality will be apparent and more palatable disguised as illusion. We often use illusion to conceal as well as to illuminate reality.*

2. *Through her illusions, which deny reality, Amanda draws needed strength to cope with the realistic present. If she were to rid herself of her illusions, she would rid herself of her own persona. She is what she is because of her illusions and without them she would be nothing. Her dreams are her life supports.*

3. *Laura, herself, and her hope are as fragile as the glass animals and as easily destroyed. Her illusions of hope have been smashed into bits when Amanda realistically calls her an unmarried cripple.*

4. *Escaping reality entirely is possible. We can, however, and often do, exchange one reality for another, one illusion for another. We can create a reality through illusion or turn a reality into illusion, but we can never viably survive without either.*

7. Ask students to select one of the works from this lesson and work in pairs to write another installment in the lives of the characters. Tell students to retain the characters' senses of reality and illusion.

Reality and Illusion in *Oedipus the King* by Sophocles

1. Oedipus lives as king of Thebes in what he sees as reality. We know that Oedipus actually lives in illusion. Has this illusion prevented Oedipus from achieving happiness?

2. Thebes is now suffering from a pestilence. Does Oedipus see this as a threat to his perception of reality or know that the cause might be his responsibility?

3. When Oedipus learns the truth, he does not hide behind ignorance but accepts the responsibility of his actions. While Jocasta kills herself in order to escape the brutal reality, Oedipus blinds himself to intensify his suffering of it. He has stripped away the illusion he once thought was reality and uncovered a horrible truth, reality itself. His self-blindness is now his reality, but in this blindness he sees as he never could before. How does Sophocles use this visual concept in presenting reality and illusion?

Name_____

Date _____

Reality and Illusion in *The Great Gatsby* by F. Scott Fitzgerald

1. In this novel, Fitzgerald describes Daisy Buchanan as the ultimate reward in Gatsby's reach toward the American dream. At one point in the novel, Gatsby, thinking he is not observed, stretches his arms toward Daisy's house. Only after Gatsby has accumulated a record of heroism, social status, wealth, and property does he deem himself worthy to begin his conquest of Daisy. We know that Daisy is incapable of a truly honest relationship and is corrupt in her gross negligence in the death of Myrtle. Why does Gatsby never realize these things about Daisy?

2. How does the advertising sign of Dr. T. J. Eckleburg, occulist, create an illusion of a supreme observer in the novel?

3. Nick Carraway, the narrator of *The Great Gatsby*, says in reference to Gatsby and Daisy's first meeting in five years, "There must have been moments even that afternoon when Daisy tumbled short of his dream—not through her own fault, but because of the colossal vitality of his illusion." How can an illusion, something unreal, generate vitality?

4. During the party which occurs in chapter 3, Jordan meets a "stout, middle-aged man, with enormous owl-eyed spectacles" in Gatsby's library. What do we learn about Gatsby in regard to reality and illusion through this encounter Jordan has with the "owl-eyed" man who has the ability to see beyond appearances?

Name_____

Date _____

Reality and Illusion in *The Glass Menagerie*
by Tennessee Williams

1. Williams's stage directions call for this play to be produced behind a transparent curtain, or scrim, and Tom Wingfield says in his opening lines, "I give you truth in the pleasant disguise of illusion." What effect does the curtain have on the play's reality, and why does Tom use illusion to disguise truth?

2. In spite of being deserted by her husband, Amanda Wingfield keeps a large picture of him in the living room. In spite of Laura's obvious shyness and inability to socialize, Amanda expects her to have gentleman callers. Yet, Amanda calls Tom a selfish dreamer at the end of the play but does not recognize the selfishness of her own dreams. Why does Williams permit this character to behave this way?

3. Laura's collection of glass animals is remembered by Tom as "bits of a shattered rainbow." The rainbow is a literary symbol of hope, relating to the arc Noah witnessed at the end of the flood. What is the reality implied in Tom's statement?

4. Tom escapes his family situation by going to the movies every night. The movies offer more illusion and further obscure reality. When Tom finally acknowledges the Wingfield family reality, he leaves, but instead of going to the movies, he roams the world as a sailor. Is escaping reality possible?

Lesson 36
Illusion and Reality in *The Wild Duck*

Objective

To explore the positive and negative effects of illusion in *The Wild Duck* and in our lives

Notes to the Teacher

Henrick Ibsen has written several plays that explore the theme of the destructive effects of illusion. In *A Doll's House*, he shows that a secure happy home may be a stifling illusion that prevents a woman from achieving maturity. In *An Enemy of the People*, he creates an illusion of safety and health that masks pollution and death for an entire community. In *The Wild Duck*, he examines the flip side of illusion, the possibility that illusion may be necessary for security and love.

Since Ibsen writes much between the lines, never oversimplifying life, the class should read *The Wild Duck* aloud, listen to a recording of it, or view a videotape of it before it is discussed. You might want to stop to explain or discuss important or obscure passages with them.

Procedure

1. Review with students their prior reading of *The Wild Duck*.

2. Distribute **Handout 70**. Divide the class into seven groups, each working on one of the roles. Groups are to choose one of their members to present their group's monologue. At the conclusion of each individual monologue, invite class members to ask questions to the group about their character's actions, motives, and feelings.

3. After the monologue presentations and discussions, conduct a class exploration of reality and illusions. Use these questions:

   a. Why, exactly, did Hedwig kill herself?

   Gregers appealed to her idealism by asking her to sacrifice the thing she loved most to regain her father's love. When she told Gregers that, after thinking it over, she was reluctant, he intimated that she was corrupted by living in "this house." After this conversation, her father rejected her twice, and Hedwig must have despaired of winning him back into her favor.

   b. How do each of the following characters respond to the "demands of the ideal?"

   Hedwig—as above

   Hjalmar—He rejects Hedwig because she may be Werle's child; he decides to move out of his own home with his father but then decides to stay because he cannot manage all the problems, especially his father's rabbits.

   Werle—After years of deceit and manipulation for his own profit, he establishes an honest relationship with Mrs. Sorby, although he does manipulate Gregers into coming home for the wedding to give Mrs. Sorby an air of respectability.

   Gina—She knows she could not have afforded the idealism of telling Hjalmar of her affair with Werle because Hjalmar would not have married her, which not only would have left Hedwig illegitimate but also would have left Hjalmar without the good practical wife he needs to find his hat, to keep the accounts, to run the photography business, and to feed the family.

   Relling—He recognizes the need for illusions and rejects Gregers's idealistic insistence on truth.

   c. What does the play say about ideals?

   The doctrinaire idealist, Gregers, cares more for his ideas than for those he says he wants to help. Therefore, living without illusions is not necessarily an absolutely worthwhile ideal.

   d. What is the function of the attic-forest in the play?

   It stands for a sustaining life-lie. It is harmless but significant to old Ekdel, who hasn't much else, and to Hjalmar, indicating his need for a life-lie. The life-lie is also important to Mulvik, who must believe he is possessed so that he can allow himself some episodes of drunkenness without too much self-hatred, and, of course, to Gina and Hedwig, whose "happiness is destroyed" as Relling predicted when the lie upon which their home is built is destroyed.

e. What is the function of alcohol in the play?

Mrs. Werle, Ekdel, and Molvik all drink to cover up reality.

f. What is the function of Mrs. Sorby in the play?

Mrs. Sorby's function is to provide a foil with Werle for the Gina-Hjalmar relationship. Mrs. Sorby and Werle have told each other all about their pasts and have a "mutual sinners' amnesty," leading to a true marriage relationship. This marriage keeps the play from saying that all relationships are based on illusions.

g. How does Hjalmar's being undeceived ironically lead to his seeing reality as illusion?

He mistrusts Hedwig's love for him and thinks she, with Gina, has planned to get Werle's money all along.

4. After the discussion, have students respond in a short piece of writing to this question: How has reading *The Wild Duck* altered your understanding of ideals, illusions, and reality?

Name_____

Date _____

What Would They Say?

Hjalmar as Deceived
> Develop the conflict between naivete and guilt in regard to your self-indulgence.

Hjalmar as Hero (Self-deceived)
> Develop the conflict between your pose as martyr and savior and your conscience as you try to undeceive yourself.

Hjalmar as Undeceived
> Develop the conflict between the real hurt you experience and the righteous indignation you feel about the injustice you protest.

Gina
> Clearly develop what lies and manipulations you have agreed to and your justification for your acts.

Old Werle
> Justify your manipulation of both Hjalmar and old Ekdel; explain why you have changed your ways lately.

Gregers
> Justify your actions toward both Hjalmar and Hedwig. What illusions about these two are shattered?

Relling
> Comment on Gregers's actions; give your philosophy of the life-lie and how it applies to both Hjalmar and Molvik; explain why you developed this philosophy.

As you prepare for the monologues, determine

    a. your primary goal in the play

    b. all your lies, white lies, manipulations, and/or rationalizations

    c. your character's attitude toward illusions and lies

Lesson 37
Luigi Pirandello's *Henry IV*

Objectives

- To have students analyze Pirandello's treatment of reality and illusion in *Henry IV*
- To enable students to relate this treatment to views in other works

Notes to the Teacher

Italian playwright Luigi Pirandello, an important voice in modern drama, focuses largely on the shifting nature of reality and the inevitability of illusion. Pirandello writes of "The construction... which each of us by means of illusion makes of himself for himself." He continues, "Do we see ourselves as we are, in our true undiluted reality, and not as we wish to be? By means of a trick world inside us, spontaneously, the product of hidden tendencies or of unconscious imitation, do we not in good faith believe ourselves different from what substantially we are? And yet we think, we work, and we live according to this fictional and even sincere interpretation of ourselves."

Many critics consider *Henry IV* Pirandello's finest play, although other plays such as *Right You Are, If You Think You Are,* and *Six Characters in Search of an Author* may be more well-known. In *Henry IV*, reality and illusion interconnect and shift. In this lesson, students examine Pirandello's interweaving of illusion and reality. They then relate the play to other literary treatments of the same topics.

You will want to obtain Pirandello's *Henry IV* and make it available to your class to read in preparation for this lesson.

Procedure

1. Have students complete **Handout 71**.

2. Review responses.

   Suggested Responses:

Real Identity	Acted Identities
An intense and theatrical person whose injury in a masquerade incident caused him a long period of insanity	Henry IV—11th century German emperor
Matilda Spina	Matilda of Tuscany Adeleide, Henry IV's mother-in-law
Frida, Matilda's daughter	Portrait of her mother as Matilda of Tuscany
Belcredi	Charles of Anjou Benedictine Monk, Friend of "Henry IV"
Dr. Genoni	Hugh of Cluny, Abbot
Charles DiNolli, nephew of Henry IV	Portrait of "Henry IV"
Ordinary men	Harold Landolph Ordulph Berthold two valets
John, the old waiter	a monk

3. Point out that part of the challenge of reading this play is the need to distinguish various illusory and real roles. Pirandello, however, goes even beyond that distinction to insist on illusions within the reality and realities within the illusion.

199

4. Have students complete **Handout 72**.

5. Conduct a brief discussion based on students' responses.

   Suggested Response:

   Pirandello seems to see illusion as deeply embedded in what we call reality. Human beings mask themselves in many ways; much of what people do is a form of masquerade. Sometimes one adopts a role that is geared toward revealing others' pretenses.

6. Discuss the fact that, of all the characters in the play, Henry IV most values the vitality of human enjoyment. Ask students why, at the end, Henry IV chooses to maintain the illusion of madness?

   This is his only shelter from the justice that would otherwise result from his killing Belcredi.

7. Ask students to relate Pirandello's views of reality and illusion to the views of Ibsen, Robinson, Hazo, Ferlinghetti, and others they have read.

Name_____

Date _____

Reality and Illusion in Pirandello's *Henry IV*

Like many other dramas, *Henry IV* includes plays within the play. The dramatic situation is based on a masquerade in which each person played a historical role. During their visits with Henry, others must play roles of figures from the eleventh century. Even the attempted cure requires acting out a role.

Within this context, each of the thirteen characters in the play has both real and illusory identities. Use this chart to diagram the characters' roles.

Real Identity	Acted Identities

Quotations from *Henry IV*

Read the following quotations, and answer the question at the end of the handout.

1. Near the beginning of *Henry IV*, Landolph says the following to the other private counsellors:

   > . . . the way we're got up, we could do a fine historical reconstruction. There's any amount of material in the story of Henry IV. But, as a matter of fact, we do nothing. We have the form without the content. We're worse than the real secret counsellors of Henry IV; because certainly no one had given them a part to play—at any rate, they didn't feel they had a part to play. It was their life. They looked after their own interests at the expense of others, sold investitures and—what not! We stop here in this magnificent court—for what?—Just doing nothing. We're like so many puppets hung on the wall, waiting for someone to come and move us or make us talk.

2. Close to the end of Act 1, Henry IV, still feigning madness, says the following to Belcredi and Matilda:

   > But we all of us cling tight to our conceptions of ourselves, just as he who is growing old dyes his hair. What does it matter if this dyed hair of mine isn't a reality for you, if it is, to some extent, for me?—you, my Lady, certainly don't dye your hair to deceive the others, nor even yourself; but only to cheat your own image a little before the looking-glass. I do it for a joke! You do it seriously! But I assure you that you too, Madam, are in masquerade, though in all seriousness.

3. A few moments later, Henry IV adds these words:

   > I feel the atmosphere of our times and the majesty of one who knows how to be what he ought to be! . . . But woe to him who doesn't know how to wear his mask, be he king or Pope.

4. In Act 2, Henry IV reveals his sanity to his private counsellors:

   > Don't you understand? Don't you see, idiot, how I treat them, how I play the fool with them, make them appear before me just as I wish? Miserable, frightened clowns that they are! And you are amazed that I tear off their ridiculous masks now, just as if it wasn't I who had made them mask themselves to satisfy this taste of mine for playing the madman.

5. A few moments later, he adds the following:

   > I know that when I was a child I thought the moon in the pond was real. How many things I thought real! I believed everything I was told—and I was happy! Because it's a terrible thing if you don't hold on to that which seems true to you today—to that which will seem true to you tomorrow even if it is the opposite of that which seemed true to you yesterday.

6. In Act 3, Henry explains the following to DiNolli, Belcredi, and the others:

> This dress which is for me the evident, voluntary caricature of that other continu-
> ous, everlasting masquerade, of which we are the involuntary puppets, when,
> without knowing it, we mask ourselves with that which we appear to be . . . ah, that
> dress of theirs, this masquerade of theirs, of course, we must forgive it them, since
> they do not yet see it is identical with themselves.

7. Henry IV goes on to say the following about his mental abilities:

> I am cured, gentlemen, because I can act the madman to perfection, here; and I do
> it very quietly. I am only sorry for you that have to live your madness so agitatedly,
> without knowing it or seeing it.

What do these quotes suggest about Pirandello's view of illusion and reality?

Lesson 38
Gustave Flaubert's *Madame Bovary*

Objective

- To use techniques of structural analysis to derive the illusion/reality theme of *Madame Bovary*

Notes to the Teacher

This lesson assumes that students have read Flaubert's *Madame Bovary*. A detailed study of *Madame Bovary* at this time offers an opportunity to demonstrate how the theory of Lesson 22 works out in practice. In addition, Flaubert's novel is a marvelous example of the destructive effects of illusion on a woman's life. Emma Bovary is a classical example of a woman whose romantic dreams make her unable to cope with her real life. Emma's story, the plot of the novel, is rather ordinary, but Flaubert has told her story in such a way that it is a masterpiece of style; it has been called the "perfect novel." Students can discover for themselves Flaubert's genius as they apply structural approaches (Lesson 22) to this novel.

As a careful examination of Flaubert's style reveals, his attitude toward his heroine is very ambivalent. He once wrote, "Madame Bovary, I am she!" His ironic style and his exaggerations of her romantic ideas reveal that one part of his mind says, "What a little fool she is!" However, another part of Flaubert is deeply sympathetic to Emma's wishes that reality could be other than it is.

Procedure

1. Distribute **Handout 73**. Divide students into five groups, and assign each group one of the five approaches.

2. Have groups share their insights.

   Suggested Responses:

   Approach One, Structural Divisions

   In each part, Emma's illusions (from the novels read in the convent, from the ball at LaVaubyessard, and from the opera at Rouen) are dashed as she encounters the reality of

her loves: Charles is a dull doctor; Rudolphe is a hard-hearted sensualist; Leon is a boy who finally matures and wants to cast off his aging mistress for a young bride.

Approach Two, Polarization of Characters

Idealists—Emma, Charles, Leon, Justin

Realists—Homais, Lheureux, Father Bournesien, Rodolphe

Idealists

Emma is self-evident from discussing structural divisions in the novel.

Charles lives under the illusion that Emma is a faithful wife until, long after her death, in three different episodes, he finds her old love letters. His illusion dies very hard. He dresses her in her white wedding gown and covers her with green velvet for her burial, perpetuating Emma's illusions for herself.

Leon's naive worship of Emma as a bride is renounced, thereby "transforming her into an extraordinary being." Upon their rediscovery of each other, his romantic sentiments are counterpointed against the experienced Emma's.

Justin worships Emma from a distance. He feels that she can do no wrong. This feeling makes him allow her entry to the pharmacy where she gets the arsenic to poison herself. Justin is the bereaved lover who haunts Emma's grave.

Realists

Homais is the middle-class entrepreneur who keeps his eye on the main chance. His attempt to gain recognition for his own newspaper articles is responsible for Charles's unsuccessful operation on Hippolyte. When his attempt to cure the beggar's blindness is unsuccessful, he has the beggar locked up in the asylum. He argues religion with the priest over Emma's coffin.

Lheureux is an even more repulsive version of Homais. He is responsible for Emma's bankruptcy; he deliberately lures her into debts for luxuries and then advises her how to steal money from Charles to pay for them.

Finally, he combines all her debts into one sum and turns it over to Vincart for collection so that he won't be blamed.

Father Bournesien is to religion what Homais and Lheureaux are to merchandising. When Emma turns to him for help in withstanding the temptation of her love for Leon, the priest tells her of his own petty troubles instead of listening to her.

Rodolphe Boulanger is the hard-hearted realist of love. As soon as he sees Emma, he knows he wants her for his mistress. He sets about seducing her with a masterful technique. However, knowing that he cannot allow her to tie him down with herself and her child, he composes a hypocritical letter breaking off their relationship.

Approach Three, Repetition of Patterns or Elements

a. The repetitive pattern of Emma's love falls into five stages: (1) illusion, (2) aspiration to a particular lover, (3) passion fulfilled, (4) satiation (of the lover, if not of Emma), (5) rejection and abandonment of Emma.

b. Early in the novel, the religious phase comes just before stage three, when Emma fights to control her impulses. Later, it comes after stage five, when Emma seeks a reason to keep on living. In both cases, religion is described as the "most beautiful of all possible dreams" and at the end she kisses the crucifix with "the most passionate love kiss she had ever given." In both cases religion is seen as an ineffectual illusion that does not affect reality.

c. The two figures are the viscount, probably only in Emma's mind, standing for illusion, and the blind beggar, standing for the despair of reality.

Approach Four, Resolution of Conflict

a. Emma justifies her extravagant living by relating it to love: first, she simply assumed that love required luxury, second, she justifies her self-indulgence as a reward for the sacrificing of her desires, i.e., her temporary giving up of Leon. In general, then, Emma feels that she must have expensive things to support her illusions of either love or duty, whichever phase she happens to be in at the time.

b. Facing bankruptcy, Emma frantically appeals to Leon, Rodolphe, Guillaumin, and Binet for money. Flaubert has very carefully arranged the sequence of appeals. First, Emma asks Leon to pawn all her valuables and to steal money from his office. Next, she appeals to Guillaumin, who suggests he will pay her for her body, a suggestion from which she recoils in horror. Then she goes to Binet, in an episode we see only through the eyes of the scandalized neighborhood gossips. Flaubert shifts his point of view here so that we see how completely tattered Emma's reputation is. When Emma finally realizes that Leon, too, has deserted her and will not appear to help her at the appointed hour, she desperately goes to Rodolphe to "sell herself." Her final rejection by her lover, in his luxurious chateau, "I don't have the money," is her ultimate humiliation and the impetus for her suicide.

c. Emma thinks she has no other choice. She cannot bear that her husband will be able to look down on her, so she never tells him of her difficulties. Both of her lovers desert her in her need. The community rejects her lifestyle and her sexual immorality. Her illusions are completely crushed.

Approach Five, Point of View

Emma's dreams are framed by the life of her cloddish husband. Charles is depicted first as a boy who is the laughingstock of his schoolmates and finally as the disillusioned husband, who again appears ridiculous as he has a drink with his wife's lover, who finds him "comical even, and a little contemptible." The circle of Emma's stages of love and disillusionment is enclosed by a larger circle of Charles's life. This encircling contains the book's ultimate irony that the woman who searches so hopelessly for love had it all the time in the arms of her husband, whom she despised: "In his, Charles's eyes, she read a love such as she had never known." Flaubert seems to say that the reality that we cannot accept may be the closest we can get to the illusion that we cannot attain.

Name_____

Date _____

Structural Approaches to the Novel *Madame Bovary*: The Emergence of the Illusion/Reality Theme

Approach One—Structural Divisions

Explain the significance of the three distinct parts of the novel in terms of the illusion/reality theme.

Approach Two—Polarization of Characters

Show how the main characters in *Madame Bovary* divide equally into those who are idealists and those who are realists.

Approach Three—Repetition of Patterns or Elements

a. Show how Emma's life, which demonstrates love based upon illusion, repeats a futile pattern.
b. Emma repeatedly turns to religion. Where is her religious phase likely to come in her life patterns? What is the thematic significance of this pattern?
c. Show how the repeated appearances of two shadowy figures near the end of the novel are tied to the illusion/reality theme.

Approach Four—Resolution of Conflict

a. How is the problem (conflict) that Emma faces at the end of the novel related to the illusion/reality theme?
b. What solutions does Emma accept? Why do we see Emma's visit to Binet through the eyes of the village gossips? Why are the various episodes of Emma's desperate search for help ordered as they are?
c. Why does Emma commit suicide? What significance does her suicide have for the illusion/reality theme?

Approach Five—Narrative Point of View

How does the device of framing Emma's story with the life of her husband, Charles, serve the illusion/reality theme?

Lesson 39
Synthesis of Reality and Illusion

Objectives

- To bring together concepts of reality and illusion
- To give students the opportunity to write on topics of this thematic concern

Notes to the Teacher

This final lesson of this thematic section allows students to synthesize the knowledge and understanding attained through the previous lessons. Since this reality/illusion is the basis of many works, it serves well as an approach to Advanced Placement examination questions.

Procedure

1. Arrange students in small groups. Distribute **Handout 74**. Assign specific questions to groups.

2. Have groups share responses.

3. Distribute **Handout 75**. These questions may be used as practice writings for the Advanced Placement examination, as the time limits necessitate speedy organization of answers. Ask students to share outlines by passing them around for others to read at the end of the time allowed.

4. Use **Handout 76** as a timed writing experience.

Questions on Reality and Illusion

1. When does illusion supply a *raison d'etre* (reason for being) for particular characters from literature?

2. What are some consequences that await characters who deny or fail to recognize reality?

3. What are some instances when characters recognize illusion but prefer to ignore it?

4. Some characters are shattered when their illusions are destroyed. Give examples.

5. How can a reader determine the credibility of a character's perception of reality?

6. How does the treatment of reality and illusion differ in fiction, drama, and poetry?

7. Why is the conflict of reality and illusion so prevalent in many works? How does it reflect daily life?

8. How do we differentiate between the realities and illusions evident in our own lives?

9. What are commonly accepted illusions that are beneficial to the common welfare?

10. What are some realities of life that one must recognize in order to achieve success?

Outlining Essay Answers

Use the simplified outline to include points you would use in writing essay answers to the questions that follow.

1. Thesis statement
2. Support
    a. Topic sentence
    b. Example
3. Support
    a. Topic sentence
    b. Example
4. Support
    a. Topic Sentence
    b. Example
5. Summarizing sentence

Allow fifteen minutes of outlining time for each question.

1. Choose a drama in which the author illustrates a character's inner conflict created by reality and illusion. Evaluate the effect this conflict has on the total work.

2. Select a novel wherein the main character's illusions directly lead to that character's failure. Explain why this failure is unavoidable.

3. Sometimes characters create illusions as defenses against realities. Select a work that illustrates this tendency, and evaluate the author's use of this approach.

Timed Writing: Reality and Illusion

Select a major work in which a character's perception of reality creates an illusion. In a well-organized essay, explain how this perception contributes to the theme of the work.

You may write for forty minutes.

Name_____

Date _____

Tips on Taking the
Advanced Placement English Examinations

When the course work is finished and the last essay is written, one question remains: What do I need to know for the Advanced Placement English examinations? The list below is a compilation of formulas that have proven successful.

1. Make very sure you understand what is called for in the question. Reread it several times, and underline key words of instruction. Pay attention to special warnings, such as "Avoid plot summary," and *heed these directions.*

2. Make a skeletal outline before you begin to write your essay answers in order to assure logical progression from thesis statement to conclusion. Keep your answer directed to the question, by using key words or key concepts in your essay. Make sure your evidence of support is relevant. Do not pad your essay with redundancy. Keep your conclusion brief, and do not belabor the points you wish to stress.

3. Store in your mind at least two twentieth-century novels of literary merit with which you are most familiar. Make sure you have clearly in your mind the titles, authors, opening paragraphs, characters, inner or outer conflicts, themes, any prominent stylistic devices, and thematic implications. Being extremely knowledgeable of two novels is much better than being slightly knowledgeable of ten.

4. Store in your mind at least two modern dramas of literary merit with which you are most familiar. Know the titles, authors, opening and closing scenes, characters, which conflicts are present, themes, production devices, and thematic implications. Make sure you select plays by different authors; Knowing one play by Ibsen and one by Williams, for instance, will be more practical than knowing two plays by one author.

5. Store in your mind at least two plays by William Shakespeare. One tragedy and one comedy or historical play would be advisable. Know the settings, major characters, rising and falling action, as well as opening and concluding scenes. Do not use terms such as "soliloquy" or "comic relief" unless you are definite in your understanding of their purpose.

6. Be confident of your reading comprehension skills in nonfiction. Read these selections carefully, and always look for main ideas, central images, allusions, point of view, and tone. Underline those lines that reveal these elements.

7. Make sure your poetic background is strong enough that you are comfortable with this genre. Include line numbers when you use them as references in your essay. Be aware of any poetic devices that may appear in the poem about which you are asked to write. Reread the poem until you feel comfortable with its meaning.

8. Come to the test location rested and mentally alert. Do not spend your final class days cramming; this approach will only add to the apprehension of the exam. Spending your time strengthening your already strong areas, is better than trying to learn new information at this point.

9. Write your answers as legibly and as intelligently as you know how. You do not want to antagonize your Advanced Placement reader with sloppy penmanship, grammar, or spelling, although these are not used in the criteria for your score.

10. Know that you are well-prepared for the test if you have done well on your class assignments. You are as capable of success as any other high-school student who is taking the test at the same moment.

Index

	Lesson Number	Handout Number		Lesson Number	Handout Number
Sophocles	16, 35		Twain, Mark	15	24, 27
Steinbeck, John	12, 21, 30, 32	17, 36, 58, 61	"Ulysses"	25	44
			"Unknown Citizen, The"	9	11, 12
Stevens, Wallace	8	10	"Use of Force, The"	1, 2	
Tempest	17	29	Vonnegut, Kurt	31	60
Tennyson, Alfred, Lord	25, 30	44, 56	Warren, Robert Penn	27	50
"The Sniper"	31		Whitman, Walt	6	8
Thomas, Dylan	12	17	*Wild Duck, The*	36	70
"Those Winter Sundays"	6	8	Wilde, Oscar	30	58
"To a Mouse"	30	58	Williams, Tennessee	35	69
To the Lighthouse	21	36	Williams, William Carlos	1	
Tolstoy, Leo	30, 32, 34	57, 61, 66	*Wise Blood*	21, 22	36, 39
Turn of the Screw, The	22	39	Woolf, Virginia	21	36
			Yevtushenko, Yevgeny	25	

Acknowledgments

For permission to reprint all works in this volume by each of the following authors, grateful acknowledgment is made to the following holders of copyright, publishers, or representatives.

Lesson 6, Handout 8
"Those Winter Sundays" by Robert Hayden from *Angle of Ascent, New and Selected Poems*, by Robert Hayden. Reprinted with the permission of Liveright Publishing Corporation. Copyright © 1975, 1972, 1970, 1966 by Robert Hayden.

"The Bean Eaters" from *The World of Gwendolyn Brooks* by Gwendolyn Brooks. Copyright © 1959 by Gwendolyn Brooks. By permission of Harper & Row Publishers, Inc.

Lesson 8, Handout 10
"Autumn Refrain" from *The Collected Poems of Wallace Stevens*. Copyright 1936 by Wallace Stevens and renewed 1964 by Holly Stevens. Reprinted by permission of Alfred A. Knopf, Inc., New York, New York.

Lesson 9, Handout 11
"The Unknown Citizen" from *W. H. Auden: Collected Poems*, edited by Edward Mendelson. Copyright 1940 and renewed 1968 by W. H. Auden. Reprinted by permission of Random House, Inc., New York, New York and Faber and Faber, London, England.

Lesson 12, Handout 17
Excerpt from *Major Barbara* by George Bernard Shaw. Reprinted by permission of The Society of Authors, London, England, on behalf of the Bernard Shaw Estate.

Excerpt form "Memories of Christmas" by Dylan Thomas from *Quite Early One Morning*. Copyright 1954 by New Directions Publishing Corporation, New York, New York. Reprinted with permission of New Directions Publishing and David Higham Associates Limited, London, England.

Excerpt form *The Fire Next Time* by James Baldwin. Copyright © 1962 by James Baldwin. A Dial Press Book reprinted by permission of Doubleday & Co., Inc., New York, New York.

Excerpt form "Battle Scene" by John Steinbeck from *The Portable Steinbeck*. Reprinted with permission from Viking-Penguin, Inc., New York, New York.

Lesson 13, Handout 19
Excerpt from *The Crack-Up* by F. Scott Fitzgerald. Copyright 1945 by New Directions Publishing Corporation, New York, New York. Reprinted with permission.

Lesson 13, Handout 21
Excerpt from "Ideals as Goals" by Edward Grant Conklin from *Man, Real and Ideal*. Copyright 1943 Charles Scribner's Sons; copyright renewed. Reprinted with the permission of Charles Scribner's Sons, New York, New York.

Lesson 15, Handout 23
"The Dark of the Moon" by Eric Sevareid from *America: 20th Century Exposition Man and the Social Machine* by David R. Weimer and Joan Myers Weimer, 1973. Copyright 1973 by Eric Sevareid. Reprinted by permission of Don Congdon Associates, Inc., New York, New York.

Lesson 15, Handout 25
Excerpt from *Process and Reality* by Alfred North Whitehead. Copyright 1929 by Macmillan Publishing Co., Inc., renewed 1957 by Evelyn Whitehead. Reprinted by permission of Macmillan Publishing Company, New York, New York.

Lesson 21, Handout 36
An excerpt from *Wise Blood* by Flannery O'Connor, 1962. Reprinted with permission of the publisher, Farrar, Straus, & Giroux, Inc., New York, New York.

Excerpt from *The Grapes of Wrath* by John Steinbeck, 1939. Published by Viking-Penguin, Inc., New York, New York.

Excerpt from *To the Lighthouse* by Virginia Woolf, 1955. Published by Harcourt, Brace, Jovanovich, New York, New York.

Lesson 21, Handout 38
Excerpt from *A Portrait of the Artist as a Young Man* by James Joyce, 1944. Published by Viking-Penguin, Inc., New York, New York.

Language Arts Series

Advanced Placement

Advanced Placement English: Practical Approaches to Literary Analysis
Advanced Placement English: In-depth Analysis of Literary Forms
Advanced Placement Poetry
Advanced Placement Short Story
Advanced Placement Writing 1
Advanced Placement Writing 2

Composition

Advanced Composition
Basic Composition
Creative Writing
Daily Writing Topics
Formula Writing 1—Building Toward Writing Proficiency
Formula Writing 2—Diverse Writing Situations
Grammar Mastery—For Better Writing, Workbook Level 1
Grammar Mastery—For Better Writing, Workbook Level 2
Grammar Mastery—For Better Writing, Teacher Guide
Journalism: Writing for Publication
Prewriting/Rewriting
Research 1: Information Literacy
Research 2: The Research Paper
Writing 1: Learning the Process
Writing 2: Personalizing the Process
Writing Short Stories
Writing Skills and the Job Search

Genres

Mythology
Nonfiction: A Critical Approach
Participating in the Poem
Science Fiction—19th Century
Short Poems: Their Vitality and Versatility
The Short Story

Literary Traditions

American Literature 1: Beginnings through Civil War
American Literature 2: Civil War to Present
Archetypes in Life, Literature, and Myth
British Literature 1: Beginnings to Age of Reason
British Literature 2: Romantics to the Present
Honors American Literature 1
Honors American Literature 2
Multicultural Literature: Essays, Fiction, and Poetry
World Literature 1
World Literature 2

Skills

Junior High Language Arts
Speech
Thinking, Reading, Writing, Speaking

Special Topic

Supervisor/Student Teacher Manual
Peer Mediation: Training Students in Conflict Resolution

The Publisher

All instructional materials identified by the TAP® (Teachers/ Authors/Publishers) trademark are developed by a national network of teachers whose collective educational experience distinguishes the publishing objective of The Center for Learning, a non-profit educational corporation founded in 1970.

Concentrating on values-related disciplines, the Center publishes humanities and religion curriculum units for use in public and private schools and other educational settings. Approximately 500 language arts, social studies, novel/drama, life issues, and faith publications are available.

While acutely aware of the challenges and uncertain solutions to growing educational problems, the Center is committed to quality curriculum development and to the expansion of learning opportunities for all students. Publications are regularly evaluated and updated to meet the changing and diverse needs of teachers and students. Teachers may offer suggestions for development of new publications or revisions of existing titles by contacting

The Center for Learning

Administrative/Editorial Office
21590 Center Ridge Road
Rocky River, OH 44116
(440) 331-1404 • FAX (440) 331-5414
E-mail: cfl@stratos.net
Web: www.centerforlearning.org

For a free catalog, containing order and price information, and a descriptive listing of titles, contact

The Center for Learning

Shipping/Business Office
P.O. Box 910
Villa Maria, PA 16155
(724) 964-8083 • (800) 767-9090
FAX (888) 767-8080